THE
SERVICE
DRIVEN™
LEADER

Moving Your People and Your Bottom Line Forward

DONALD CLINEBELL

Published by HigherLife Development Services, Inc.

PO Box 623307

Oviedo, Florida 32762

(407) 563-4806

www.ahigherlife.com

ISBN 978-1-7326377-0-2

First Edition

Printed in the United States of America

Praise for
The Service Driven Leader

"I love this book! Donald Clinebell has given us a truly uplifting work that should be read by all leaders who desire to create a unified and highly motivated workforce focused on their organization's success. *The Service Driven Leader* provides a guide on how leaders who serve and care for others will create a culture that will empower and energize employees to help stimulate continuous improvement while increasing profits. In his book, Clinebell delivers important advice, which is to tell employees that they are valued, but first leaders should learn to value themselves. He also provides a stimulating and instructional message on how to transform ourselves by being service-driven leaders, who will be of benefit to the organization we serve while strengthening relationships with fellow employees, family, and friends."

—Alan Adamo

Former Corporate Vice President of Human Resources,
Fluidmaster
Organizational Development Instructor, University of California, Irvine

"*The Service Driven Leader* is a compelling work, an instant classic. Donald Clinebell applies the concept of servant leader to the private sector in a ground-breaking way. He crafts a powerful daily tool for the creation of an inspired, motivated, and productive leadership team and work force. *The Service Driven Leader* is a must-read for business leaders who want to move their people and their bottom line forward!"

—Paul Barnes

Former Production Superintendent

Shell Oil Company

"I have been 'in service' with Donald for the past twenty years. He is a passionate servant with an engaging and powerful message."

—Mitch Ritschel

Senior Living Industry Executive

"*The Service Driven Leader* by Donald Clinebell demonstrates an amazingly simple yet potentially life-changing shift in the paradigm of modern business. The capacity for a service-driven life is within us all, and as he aptly points out, is a uniting force. Donald demonstrates a unique vision to energize and focus the leadership of any organization, large or small, to 'move the bottom line forward,' in his words, and help us all become better versions of ourselves. He demonstrates this with real-life examples and an easy-to-follow methodology."

—Susan Hattan, JD

Estate Planner

Susan Dallas Hattan Law Firm

"Much has been written on compassionate management, servant leadership, and corporate culture in business. Donald Clinebell's latest book, *The Service Driven Leader: Moving Your People and Your Bottom Line Forward*, is a practical application that goes beyond. It addresses the true meaning of being an effective leader through humility and inspiring others to drive organizations to greater performance and true meaning."

—Vince Bianco

Interim CEO and Senior Sales Leader

Vince Bianco LLC

Former Chief Executive Officer, Advance Medical Reviews

"Ground-breaking and empowering! *The Service Driven Leader* is a must-read for every business leader; it is practical in its application and inspiring in its approach. Many people go through work life just barely surviving, without passion and joy for their jobs, especially in the legal field. This book is about finding passion in work through service to your clients and customers, which ultimately comes back to empower you and your business. Whatever your work background, Donald Clinebell's service-focused approach is going to make your life better, motivate and engage your employees, and move your bottom line forward."

—Anabella Q. Bonfa, JD

Wellman & Warren LLP

Acknowledgments

Over the past five years, I've been blessed with the opportunity to speak about my books all over the country. I have related time and again my own story: how I came to know the power of service to change and renew the lives of those I serve and the power of service to change and renew and empower…me.

In *Extraordinary Living*, I wrote about service as the "common thread" that crosses all lines and boundaries and unites us all. That common thread is the central component that runs through all five major religions and all belief systems of consequence, from agnosticism to New Age philosophy to science-based thinking.

The Service Driven Leader is the final book in the "Service Driven" trilogy. It is a book that has been on my mind and in my heart for two decades. It is the application of the concepts of how service, of servant leadership, relates to business leadership.

I attended a dinner party recently at which one of the guests, the CEO of a large company, had heard about what was then my upcoming book on service-driven leadership. He asked this question: "I've heard great things from several of my colleagues who have read the flyer about your new book. They're using words like 'revolutionary' and 'groundbreaking.' What's the excitement about?"

For me, the excitement is this: when the power of service

is applied to business leadership, it engages and inspires; it moves and changes companies. Service-driven leadership gives companies the power to shape their financial future. Indeed, one service-driven leader can change a company from the inside out…and carry it to greatness, in every way.

I am grateful to the many friends, colleagues, and business leaders who have been with me on this service-driven journey. I extend my great thanks to David Welday for his continuing dialogue and input. David's contributions, and his commitment to ideas that truly matter, cannot be overstated.

There are many who have supported this journey over the years:

- Sponsors and supporters of the Service Driven Institute and Service Driven Seminar

- My friend and fellow man of service, Paul Barnes, who has contributed in many ways to the mission of the Service Driven Institute

- In the Company of Prayer and its dynamic founder and president, Leslie Bianco

- The Shoffner Law Firm, the Susan Dallas Hattan Law Offices, and San Clemente Bath Company, who have all been of support and encouragement along the way

- Loyal and dedicated supporters of the Institute

- "Launching Sponsors" of the Service-Driven Leadership Seminars

My wonderful children, whom I love so dearly, have continued to be an important part of this journey. Both have had an essential role in shaping my view of the power of service in all our lives. I am grateful today, and every day, for their love and for who they are and are becoming. Their extraordinary lives bless and enrich mine daily.

My great thanks to Libbye Morris, whose editing skills and input both on this book and on *Extraordinary Living* went "above and beyond."

I look forward to seeing you at an upcoming Service-Driven Leadership Seminar in your area. In the meantime, feel free to communicate with me at theservicedrivenlife@gmail.com or through the Service Driven Institute website (www.servicedriveninstitute.com).

In love and service,

Donald Clinebell

San Clemente, CA, USA

Table of Contents

Introduction:
The Missing Ingredient

"If you want to build a boat, don't begin by collecting wood, cutting boards, or assigning tasks. Begin by awakening in the souls of your workers a longing for the vast and boundless sea."

—*Antoine de Saint-Exupery*

A serious problem is plaguing the American workforce, robbing employees of fulfilling careers and organizations of productivity:

As business leaders, we are all, in a sense, boat builders.

---

disengagement. You could call it apathy, which is defined as a lack of interest or concern.

If you are a business leader in a boat- or ship-building company, the powerful quotation from Saint-Exupery shown above is a literal statement, a literal guide to creating engaged and productive leaders and employees. But if you are not a boat builder in the literal sense, this is a metaphor—a very powerful one. As business leaders, we are all, in a sense, boat builders.

Saint-Exupery uses a metaphor for awakening in your workers and employees a powerful and productive force: "the longing in their souls." What they long for is not literally "the vast and boundless sea." Rather, they long for purpose, meaning, joy, and fulfillment in what they do. If they don't get those important needs met in your company, they will constantly be looking for them elsewhere, at some level, in other companies. They will leave your company to go wherever they can find them—or think they can find them.

The Problem: Only One-Third of American Workers Are Engaged

According to Gallup's 2017 "State of the American Workplace" report, only 30 percent of employees are what Gallup calls engaged at work—involved in, enthusiastic about, and committed to their work and workplace. They love their jobs and make their organizations and America better every day. At the other end of the spectrum, 16 percent of employees are actively disengaged—they are miserable in the workplace and destroy what the most engaged employees build. The remaining 51 percent of employees are not engaged; they're just there.[1]

---

1   "State of the American Workplace," Gallup, 2017, https://news.gallup.com/reports/199961/7.aspx. This is the third iteration of the study, which Gallup developed using data collected from more than 195,600 US employees via the Gallup Panel and Gallup Daily tracking in 2015 and 2016, and more than 31

Gallup measures employee engagement using a twelve-element survey (Gallup's Q12) rooted in employees' performance-development needs. When those needs are met, employees become emotionally and psychologically attached to their work and workplace. As a result, their individual performance soars, and they propel their teams and organizations to improved crucial outcomes such as higher levels of productivity, safety, and quality.[2]

Engaged employees benefit their organizations and the economy as a whole. The Gallup report says, "The real goal of employee engagement is improved business outcomes. Engaged employees contribute to the economic health of their company and the nation in ways that other employees do not. Employees who are engaged are more likely to stay with their organization, reducing overall turnover and the costs associated with it. They feel a stronger bond to their organization's mission and purpose, making them more effective brand ambassadors. They build stronger relationships with customers, helping their company increase sales and profitability."

The Gallup study also reveals that more than half (51 percent) of employees are searching for a new job or watching for openings elsewhere.[3]

If your company is one of those wracked by disengaged and unmotivated employees, the chance of your company growing, or

---

million respondents through Gallup's Q12 Client Database.

2   Ibid.

3   Ibid.

even of surviving, in the long term is slim. Selfish employees—those who watch out for themselves—have produced a business model and environment that does not work. It is fundamentally dysfunctional.

The Solution: Service-Driven Leadership

This book is about a revolutionary and groundbreaking solution for the disengagement problem: service-driven leadership. As Stephen Covey points out, "The great leader is seen as servant first, and that simple fact is the key to his/her greatness."[4] Part of

---

Part of the greatness of service-driven leaders is their ability to produce engaged employees.

---

the greatness of service-driven leaders is their ability to produce engaged employees—those who are inspired and motivated—and involved in, enthusiastic about, and committed to their work and to their company's vision and future.

Service-driven leadership is leadership that puts serving

---

4   As stated in the foreword to Robert K. Greenleaf, Servant Leadership: A Journey into the Nature of Legitimate Power & Greatness, 25th Anniversary Edition (Malwah, New Jersey: Paulist Press, 2002).

others first—employees, clients, customers, community. When leadership meets the power of service, it engages and inspires; it moves and changes people and thus companies. Outlook changes outcomes. And, as you will see in this book, it gives companies the power to shape their financial future.

If you've heard the term "servant leader" before, perhaps you think it refers to someone leading a service organization such as a Rotary Club, a Kiwanis Club, or a Junior League Club—a nonprofit, 501(c)(3) organization. Or perhaps you think of Mother Teresa, who said, "I live as a servant, and thereby I am changed, I am renewed."

This is certainly one part of the "servant leader" concept. The power of service transforms and empowers charitable organizations. But if you leave it at that, you will have missed an extraordinary opportunity! I say this because being a servant leader is not only personally transformative; it is a highly effective business practice.

My second book, *Extraordinary Living*, published in 2016, is a study of the power of service in all our lives, in every part of our lives—across all boundaries of faith and no-faith, all belief systems, and all spiritual disciplines of significance.

This book, *The Service Driven Leader*, is a companion to *Extraordinary Living*. It applies the power of service in the context of business and business leadership. It is intended for leaders and aspiring leaders in profit-based companies who seek to understand and apply servant leadership in a way that is specific and revolutionary and will ensure enduring success. I wrote it for leaders who want to remove the limits on their capacity to lead entirely.

If you wish to super-charge the performance of your business or organization and ensure its enduring success, I challenge you to enrich and expand your thinking about "service." This book is about leadership that comes not just from the head but from the heart. When leadership comes out of service, it is powerful, productive, and inspired. It is leadership that changes companies and businesses forever—moving people, and thus products and services.

As a leader, you want to make those around you better. As a service-driven leader, you have the opportunity, but more importantly, the *potential* to make your entire organization better—your employees, your profits, even your community. Service-driven leaders understand the power of service to change and renew others—and themselves.

Service is the missing ingredient in the American workforce.

In the pages that follow, we will explore how to incorporate service-driven leadership to your organization. When you make the choice to serve—when you engage in service as a business leader—you will discover the ability and the power to shape the future of your company. You will have made a choice that represents the deciding point between a company's enduring success and its eventual demise.

By reading this book, you are seizing an opportunity to

accomplish some extraordinary things:

1. Re-engage and empower yourself in your chosen profession.

2. Engage your employees in *what* they do and *why* they do it.

3. Change your company, business, employees, and community, for the better—forever.

The reward is that you will be able to satisfy that longing for fulfillment in your own soul and in the souls of those who work with you toward a common purpose. And when that happens, there are literally no limits to increased productivity and moving your company's bottom line forward.

Chapter 1

Seize the Opportunity

"Opportunity is missed by most people because it comes

dressed in overalls and looks like work."

—*Thomas Edison, holder of 1,309 US patents*

One winter night a few years ago, I flew into Phoenix, Arizona. On that clear night, as we approached the airport in final descent, I saw down below a grid of city lights that seemed to extend to the horizon and beyond. It was beautiful in a strange way, and breathtaking.

I thought of the man who invented the light bulb, Thomas Edison. In his lifetime, Edison had seen from a sixth story window of a run-down building in New York City a small grid, a block or two, of lights spread out before him. I couldn't help wondering what Edison would think and say if he had been sitting next to me on that plane that night.

Thomas Edison was an accomplished man with 1,309 patents, many of which changed history—the light bulb, the phonograph, and the telegraph. Late in his life, Edison was asked a simple question: "Why did you work so hard and push yourself so hard?"

What looked like work became an opportunity to succeed and to serve.

His answer: "It was fun." Then he added, "I am in service. The technology I found and invented will not be fully utilized till long after I am gone."

Edison, a man of science and business, was a service-driven

leader. What looked like work became an opportunity—many opportunities to succeed and to serve. He found in his work purpose, meaning, fulfillment, and yes, joy. He thereby achieved great success and literally changed the world.

As you begin to study the power of service, I encourage you to seize the opportunity before you. Before you transform the way you lead your business, begin in Chapter 2 to know extraordinary living—the power of service to change and renew others and the power of service to change, renew, and empower...you. When we understand that power in our lives, we can apply the power of service to our leadership—with amazing results.

In Chapter 3, we begin to seize the opportunity to apply the power of service—the empowerment found in extraordinary living—to our leadership as business men and women. We do that in specific and practical ways. And, as Saint-Exupery said, it's not about "collecting wood, cutting boards, or assigning tasks."

Instead, we re-energize and empower ourselves in our chosen vocations and professions. We begin to move beyond "boss" to "leader." The two are not the same. And neither your leadership team nor your employees will see you as a leader until you learn to serve. As Robert Greenleaf put it, "The great leader is seen as a servant first, and that simple fact is the key to his [or her] greatness." Put another way, if service is missing, greatness is also missing.

In this book, we, in a very real sense, apply in our business leadership the missing ingredient and see the very tangible, practical, and long-lasting results. We do this through a series of specific questions and breakout sessions designed to focus us on service-driven leadership and a series of questions focusing us on the specific keys to success as service-driven leaders. (See Appendices 1 and 2.) You can answer these focus questions in a facilitated setting (breakout sessions and focus groups) or in guided self-study.

We conclude by setting out in very specific terms your vision, your goals to implement that vision, and specific action items you can use now, including action-item completion dates. (See Appendix 3.)

At the back of this workbook, you will find ten pages available for notetaking, where you can write down ideas and concepts that inspire, motivate, and move you—or that simply make great sense for your company. Any time you have an idea about something that needs to be done in your company, or about a restatement of your vision for your company or goals that need setting—action items that now seem clear—write them down immediately. Gather and assemble them, whether in the Notes section of the workbook, in your own "service-driven" notebook, or on an electronic device of your choice. You then return to those Notes time and again, as you need to.

Let's seize the opportunity and begin moving your people and your bottom line forward. Right now!

Chapter 2

The Power of Service

""A man starts to live when he can live outside himself."
—Albert Einstein

S elf-help gurus have it all wrong. It's not all about me. It's not about endless self-analysis and ruminating about me. It's not about fifteen years of therapy.

I do agree that to live extraordinary lives, we need to learn to love ourselves unconditionally. In some ways, that's the basis of the field of psychotherapy. Self-love frees us.

To do what? To ruminate some more about *ourselves?* No.

We self-examine so we can step *outside* ourselves, loving and serving others. In doing this, we find deep meaning and great joy—true empowerment—for ourselves. *And that is extraordinary living...*

Baby Boomers: The First "Me" Generation

I come from a generation of baby boomers. We were and are a troubled generation, although we started with great optimism. We thought we had the answers, usually found in a Beatles song. ("All you need is love" "It's getting better all the time." "We hope someday you'll join us, and the world will be as one.") Not quite that simple, was it? Some baby boomers turned to drugs and alcohol, cynicism, or clinical depression. Ultimately, we became an unhappy generation. We became the first "me" generation.

Whether you agree or disagree, imagine a world in which service comes first, a world filled with men and women living in service to others, in every part of their lives. Men and women learning, in the words of Albert Einstein, "to live outside of themselves."

What would that world be like? Imagine what your world be like when you learn a simple truth: that we begin to understand the meaning of human life when, as Canadian farmer Nelson Henderson suggested, we plant trees under which we know full well we will never sit! What would your life be like if you were to plant shade trees under which you know full well you will never sit? What would the life of those around you be like?

Let's be honest. Sometimes we simply don't want to serve. Sometimes we don't want to plant shade trees. My time is pretty valuable—full up with kids, work, and, of course, drama. Sometimes, I want that "me" time. If I have to decide what to do on a Sunday afternoon—work a food drive for a local charity or sit in my easy chair and watch a ball game—the ball game usually is my first choice.

Service is a little wedge of the pie. Life fills the remainder of the pie.

Service Is the Key to Extraordinary Living

The premise of my book *Extraordinary Living* is that *service is not an add-on to life*. Rather, it is the foundation and the core…of what? Of meaning, purpose, fulfillment, worthiness, peace, and boundless joy. *That's all.*

The "Me Circle"

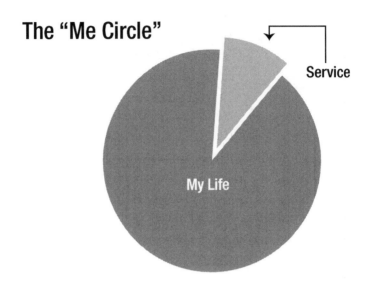

Service

My Life

Service is the key to extraordinary living. The "service-driven circle" puts service at the center of the circle and of a life in which we realize that everything we do is or can be a vessel for service.

True service begins in the home and with family. Don't take my word for it. Take the word of Mother Teresa. Why does service begin in the home? Because how we are at home and with family is exported to the rest of our lives and to our communities—including the way we interact with our neighbors, both literal and figurative.

What we do in the home inevitably works its way into our work—the place where we spend the substance of our days. If we're not "of service" in our vocations—even just in orientation and mind-set—can we ever be truly service-driven leaders?

Service Must Be at the Center of Our Lives

Given all our commitments in life—home and family, work, and neighbors—service must be at the center.

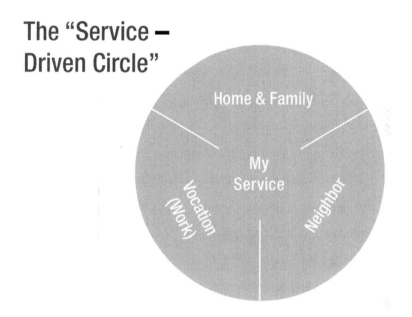

The "Service – Driven Circle"

Home & Family

My Service

Vocation (Work)

Neighbor

Service belongs in the center of the circle because it is the common thread of meaning that crosses all boundaries. Service is a central component in all major religions, all belief systems of consequence. It's a values-based common thread, really, among Christianity, Hinduism, Islam, Buddhism, Judaism, New Age philosophy, Eastern mysticism, belief in a Higher Power or source, agnosticism, and atheism.

People who are known for their lives of service sum up the importance of service in these quotes:

- **Christianity**—Mother Teresa said, "I live as a servant... and thereby I am changed; I am renewed."

- **Hinduism**—Gandhi said, "The best way to find yourself is to lose yourself in service to others." (The baby boomers, for the most part, have never figured this out.)

- **Science-based thinking**—Einstein said, "A man begins to live when he learns to live outside himself."

- **Albert Schweitzer**, a theologian, said, "The only man with any chance of happiness is the man who finds a way to serve."

- **New Age philosophy**—Wayne Dyer said, "How may I serve? Asking this question can turn your life around."

- **Agnostic thinking**—Vincent Bugliosi, a service-driven lawyer and agnostic, said, "The Golden Rule is the value base upon which all other moral codes of living are based."

- **Abraham Lincoln**—Yes, Lincoln's speeches contained many references to God. But the story of the drafting of the Gettysburg Address reveals a struggle within Lincoln—a struggle resolved by a desire to serve: "When I do good, I feel good. When I do bad, I feel bad. That's all the religion I need." Service, for Lincoln, rested on a values-based platform, on values-based spirituality.

Service-driven leadership is about aligning what is important to you in the way you live your life with something bigger than yourself, a higher purpose. The common thread found in service is nothing less than a universal human search for purpose and meaning:

"I discovered that people are not really afraid of dying; they're afraid of not ever having lived, not ever having deeply considered their life's higher purpose, and not ever having stepped into that higher purpose, and at least tried to make a difference in this world."

—*Joseph Jaworski*

Toward the end of his life, Einstein was asked, "Who among us makes the greatest contribution to humanity?" He answered, "He who brings out of love a cup of water to a thirsty man."

And the beneficiary of that act? The man who brings the cup! Why is what Einstein said so true? Because he who brings the cup—he who aligns what is important in life by the way he lives, in service, with a higher purpose—is committed to something bigger than himself. Something bigger than me! That always produces great meaning and purpose...and great joy.

Three Elements of a Service-Driven Life

Accepting the fact that service should be central to all aspects of life is the first step. But how do you achieve that? What does it look like? Below are three elements of a service-driven focus: silence, stories, and stepping outside yourself. Let's look at each one of these in detail.

1. **Silence**—Matthew Kelly, a true "revolutionary" in church thinking, coined the phrase "the classroom of silence." Be

still. Reflect, meditate, and if it's a part of your spirituality, pray. Ask yourself this question: "What is really important in life?" Most of us don't ask the question, much less find

---

Reflect, meditate, and if it's a part of your spirituality, pray.

---

the answer—or perhaps we simply don't think about it till it's too late. Caught up as we are in the business of life, we miss the question, as well as the answer: "What's important is to serve others."

Whether you are of faith, no faith, agnostic, or atheist, it's a simple exercise, a simple analysis. Get quiet. That's where the answers to most spiritual questions are found. Step into the classroom of silence, and be still for a time. Then and only then, ask yourself what feels right. Very quickly, you'll know in your heart…and you will have gone a long way toward finding yourself in this sometimes crazy world. As Jaworski says, we all are afraid of never finding a higher purpose, never finding something bigger than ourselves. It doesn't have to be that way. Choose love over fear—love and service over fear. Go there now.

2. **Stories of service, meaning, love, and joy**—Anecdotes are all around us, every day. What might appear at first glance

to be anecdotal is simply a fundamental truth—objective and quantifiable. The fundamental truth is this: when we put love and service together, the power of service changes lives—the lives of those we serve and our own lives.

A young mother in India, age twenty-nine, was blind from birth. She had two children: a six-year-old boy and a four-year-old girl. A surgeon from the United States took the time and energy to care. Working through a service club in India, the surgeon gathered and sent surgical instruments and equipment to India and assembled a surgical team of volunteers. On a January day, the surgical team flew some eight thousand miles from the United States to India to perform, without charge, an amazing and life-changing surgery.

The surgery was delicate, risky, and difficult. After ten hours of surgery and hours upon hours of recovery, the mother slowly opened her eyes and wept—not because she could see for the first time, but because for the first time ever, she laid eyes upon her son and daughter, ages six and four.

Both the young mother and the surgeon cried tears of joy. The surgeon later wrote this: "I believe I know how the surgery changed that young mother, and those two children. But what I know without doubt is that I am changed, I am renewed. In that moment, this man of science and medical expertise found a higher power. I do what I do with God's help. And in that mother and in those children, I have seen the face of God."

Where love and service are present, there is meaning, and there is joy.

Always! Without fail!

Stories of love and service are all around us. Powerful stories, miraculous stories, stories of joy. Here's another.

A service club adopted a residential school for the deaf in southern Mexico. Most of the kids have been abandoned by their parents and now live full time at the school, which has dormitories for kids ages three to seventeen. Many of the children have never experienced Christmas. Imagine their excitement and joy as the service-club members delivered beautifully wrapped gifts to those children and encouraged them to open them and enjoy the toys inside. Imagine if you were one of the people on that mission. Look in the eyes of a child in that orphanage in Mexico, a child who had never received a Christmas present—*until there was you.* The impact on the child is clear. What about the impact on you? Is there joy, purpose, and meaning for you? Deep meaning and great joy in those served and in those who serve? There is no doubt. The evidence is all around us, every day, in every part of our lives—including in our vocations.

3. **Stepping outside yourself**—I included many stories of service in my book *Extraordinary Living*. Here are two.

A Lawyer Steps outside Himself[1]

I know a very good and successful lawyer who is also a juggler. He rides a unicycle and juggles at the same time. He has an "act" that is very unlawyerlike and very funny. It would be stand-up comedy if the juggler weren't sitting down on a unicycle during the act. He performed his "act" mostly for family. One day, this lawyer/juggler was invited to take his act to a local retirement home. He wasn't sure about it. Why would anybody there want to see him do his act?

But he did it; he unicycled and juggled for a hundred seniors, complete with a quite wonderful stream of commentary and bad jokes. He had a ball, and so did the crowd! They smiled, roared with laughter, and cheered. And cheered some more. For those moments in time, the lawyer/juggler brought great joy to a place not always joyful. To a place filled with stories of loneliness and pain, he brought a great gift of love and service to neighbors, as a neighbor. The lawyer served. The lawyer stepped outside himself.

And what happened to him? Now he entertains a full circuit of senior homes and facilities. The lawyer was changed, the lawyer was renewed, and the servant was empowered.

This next story is a very personal one about the power of service in every part of our lives.

---

1 . Donald Clinebell, *Extraordinary Living: The Hidden Power That Answers Life's Most Compelling Question* (Oviedo, Florida: HigherLife Publishing, 2016), 124–25.

A Son Steps outside Himself[2]

My father was in the last year of his life. He was not well. Parkinson's disease had robbed him of the ability to do all the things he so loved to do, including writing, preaching, and teaching.

One evening, I sat at his bedside, as I did many nights in those last days. As I sat, I helped Dad with his supper. And I shared with him what I believed was in me to write. I found myself describing to him a book about a life—a life centered around, and driven by, service. A life driven by service to others in every part of that life: through home and family, through vocation, and in service to "neighbor." My own story, really. From despair to hope, from darkness to light, from sadness to great joy! A story of change and renewal.

My father listened, nodding gently, but did not speak. As we finished supper, the gloaming turned to dark, and we sat together

I knew it was precious time—time that would not come again.

in the quiet. Famous fathers are not home a lot when their kids are growing up, and I had developed some resentment about

2 . Ibid, 187–88.

that. But that evening, I found myself in the middle of what was precious time. I knew it was precious time—time that would not come again. And I knew it was time for forgiveness. I said to my father, "Dad, I love you, and I forgive it all." He nodded but didn't speak.

I read to Dad from a favorite daily reader. As he dozed off to sleep, I prepared to depart for the night. But as I turned toward the door of the room, Dad stirred and waved to me to return. I did. He had a tear in his eye. I was startled, having never seen my father cry (he was eighty-three at the time). He smiled at me and said only this: "Donald, you must write that book." I didn't understand, really, but I liked what he had said, and I lingered. A few minutes later, I once again started for the door. He called me back and pointed to a chair by his bed. I sat. The tear in his eye was now on his cheek as he, haltingly in the midst of the Parkinson's, said this: "Thank you for being here and for loving me. I love you, son. And…thank you for…*forgiving* me."

What had happened? I did my best to serve my father at the end of his life. I did so imperfectly. But the resentment dropped away as I became of service. It was in that time and in the midst of that service that he spoke to me in a way I never thought possible, in a way and in a moment every son dreams about. That moment would not have happened had I not first been of service, had I not deliberately stepped outside myself and embraced him in love and service. That's what extraordinary living is all about.

We are back to where we started. Do you want to live an extraordinary life? If so, deliberately and intentionally step outside yourself. Does joy seem far away? Purpose and meaning remote? Serve. Step outside yourself, empty of ego. And remember that

---

Step outside yourself, empty of ego.

---

where love and service are present, without exception, there is deep meaning, purpose, and empowerment. And there is great joy.

You see, the question of service is not a question; it is an answer. And whether you live in service with a faith base, a spiritual base, or a values base, the power of service is the same. The power to change and renew others? Certainly. But more than that…the power to change, and renew…and empower…*you.*

Purpose, meaning, joy, wholeness, fulfillment, worthiness, peace…cometh not in the morning. They cometh now, if you will only embrace them. Not tomorrow—today. Now. Go in service…and watch what happens!

Next, we will explore the six keys to success as a service-driven leader.

Chapter 3

Energy and Vision
Drive Leadership

"A man starts to live when he can live outside himself."

—*Albert Einstein*

Now it is time to *apply* the power of service—the empowerment found in service and extraordinary living—to our leadership as businessmen and women. We do that in specific and practical ways. And, as Saint-Exupery said, it's not about "collecting wood, cutting boards, or assigning tasks."

Instead, we must reenergize and empower ourselves in our chosen vocations and professions. In a very real sense, it is time to apply in our business leadership *the missing ingredient* and to see the very tangible, practical, and long-lasting results.

The business/corporate world is made up of leaders. Some have a theory of leadership, and some don't. Many years ago, when asked about his theory of leadership, Bill Hewlett of Hewlett-Packard fame said, "I don't know. I don't think I have a theory of leadership." That's likely why HP had to reinvent itself fundamentally when Hewlett and Packard were no longer a part of HP. Neither had made his mark beyond the spreadsheet. Neither had found or added the missing ingredient. Neither had made the choice to serve.

Let's look at how you can create enormous positive energy, empower your key leadership, increase your employee satisfaction and retention; build your brand, generate publicity that results in more customers and clients, and reduce your marketing expenses—all while increasing your team's effectiveness. We can call this a theory of leadership, or we can simply call it the keys to success…as a service-driven leader.

Let's look at a classic, but aging, definition of leadership. It is useful, but it doesn't have the "missing ingredient"—service:

Energy + Vision = Leadership

This is indeed a classic definition. It's been around for a very long time. It was the one I lived by for years —in the law firm of fifty lawyers I managed, as a leader in Rotary International, as a leader in my church, and in other leadership capacities. And this formula does bring some success. If you have energy and vision and you communicate them, you can't help but lead. Leadership is nothing more, nothing less, than guiding your team down a path, all the while communicating why that path is important, as opposed to another path, or still another path.

Energy Is Passion

Energy is listed first in this formula. Why? Because it is

Energy comes from a belief in what we are doing.

---

absolutely critical to good leadership. This is not about being loud or hyper, although if you hear me speak, I might appear to be both. It's not even enthusiasm. In this context, the word "energy" is closer to the word "passion." Energy comes from a belief in what we are doing. That is its heart. Servant leadership—service-driven leadership—as we'll see in a minute, provides an enormous reservoir to draw on, a reservoir of belief in what we are doing.

The phrase "servant leadership" originated in the works of Robert K. Greenleaf. In 1977, Greenleaf published *Servant Leadership*, a ground-breaking work that "explored the nature of legitimate power and greatness." Greenleaf's 1977 work was followed by *The Power of Servant Leadership*, a collection of Greenleaf's essays on servant leadership and on the concepts of spirit and wholeness.

Greenleaf's seminal work, *Servant Leadership*, introduced the phrase into our vocabulary, along with the principle that service ought to be the distinguishing characteristic of leadership. Businesses, Greenleaf said, would thereby be better and stronger, and servant leaders would find greater joy in their lives.

To truly embody servant leadership requires energy. Merriam-Webster defines "energy" as "a dynamic quality; the capacity of acting or being active; a usually positive spiritual force; vigorous exertion of power; usable power."

Energy is uplifting: "Good morning, everybody. Welcome. I'm glad you are here!" Positive energy is contagious, and it begets more positive energy. People want to be around it!

Communicate with energy and passion, and you'll get your company moving.

Wisdom Is the Capacity to Imagine

Now let's talk about the *vision* part of the classic formula "energy + *vision* = leadership." What is vision? It's a much-misused word. But it's not a mystery. Here is the best definition

---

The goals we set in an organization have very little meaning if they're not set in the context of a vision for the company

---

of vision I've ever heard: "Wisdom is the ability to imagine and foresee what could be." That definition turns you into a true visionary.

Often in the business world, we focus on setting and reaching goals. Vision is a broader concept than goals. The goals we set in an organization have very little meaning if they're not set in the context of a *vision* for the company or business. Where does this year fit into last? And the years before that? And future years? Seeing where your company has been, where it is, and where it's going is a critical component of leadership.

Your team's goal for this year might be to increase sales by

20 percent. But what is the *vision*? Financial stability for the company, or perhaps increased dividends. The vision defines why the goal is important.

"Energy plus vision" is, in some ways, an adequate formula for leadership. But it isn't enough! Standing alone, it is profoundly limited. Something is missing. It's like a house built without a foundation. At the first rain, flood, and wind, the house will fall.

We must take our blinders off. We must discover that without service-driven leadership, we have profoundly limited our capacity to lead, our growth and leadership potential, and the productivity of our companies and businesses. Let's look at, and add, the missing ingredient.

In the next six chapters, we will explore six keys to service-driven leadership.

Chapter 4

Key #1—Choose to Serve

*"The choice to serve is not an action in the normal sense—
it's not something you do, but an expression of your being."*

—Joseph Jaworski

The choice to serve: it is an inspiring, moving, inspirational choice. Without it, our capacity to lead is profoundly limited. The most important choice a leader makes is the choice to serve. The choice to change and empower ourselves as people and as leaders, and thereby to change the lives of those we serve: employees, clients, customers, the community, and beyond. It's very simple. When leadership meets the power of service, it engages and inspires—it moves and changes people and thus companies. The bottom line: we shape a new, exciting, and unlimited future for our companies and businesses.

In his book, *Synchronicity*, Joseph Jaworski writes that Greenleaf said this: "The first and most important choice a leader makes is the choice to serve, without which one's capacity to lead is profoundly limited. That choice is not an action in the normal sense—it's not something you do, but an expression of your being."[1]

Jaworski took that a step further when he wrote, "The most essential leadership capacity of our time is the choice to serve; when we make that choice, we discover the ability to collectively shape our future."[2]

That's the ability to shape the future in our own lives and in our businesses, both locally and globally.

Four Principles of Service-Driven Leadership

---

1 . Joseph Jaworski, *Synchronicity: The Inner Path of Leadership* (San Francisco: Berrett-Koehler Publishers, Inc., 2011), 1.

2 . Ibid, 55.

"The great leader is seen as servant first, and that simple fact is the key to his [or her] greatness." —Robert K. Greenleaf

But what exactly does a servant leader, a service-driven leader, look like? He or she is a leader who has fused two roles: servant and leader. This is, at its heart, leadership that puts serving others first: employees, clients, customers, patients, and community. When that happens, *outlook changes outcomes.*

Let's start with that most frustrating study and statistic mentioned earlier. In most profit-based companies, more than 70 percent of employees identify as "not fully engaged." That alone is often the most devastating problem and issue in troubled or underperforming companies. As a leader in your company, you have the power to change that.

Purpose, meaning, joy, and fulfillment are on full display at the top!

When we make the choice to serve, we discover the ability to shape the future collectively —our company's future and our own future. It is in this sense that effective leadership—leadership that engages both leaders and employees—comes not just from the head, but from the heart. And when it does, leadership becomes powerful, productive, inspired leadership. It moves people, it engages people, and thus it moves products and services.

Why does this work? Because purpose, meaning, joy, and fulfillment are on full display at the top! They change you first, and then they change the experience of your key leaders and your employees. The business, like you, begins to focus on purpose, meaning, joy, fulfillment, and worthiness. Energy abounds. Focus and engagement improve. A sense of joint purpose and meaning develops. Creativity and imagination blossom. Outcomes change. Bottom lines improve.

And it's all happening from the top down, from you, from the leader who understands the power of service-driven leadership to change, renew, and empower. You become the leader who understands and acts on four fundamental principles of service-driven leadership:

1. **Examine what you do and how you do it.** What goes on between your ears about your work? Do you think of yourself as worthy? Do you think of yourself as good at what you do? Do you look for the good in what you do? Or do you focus on what I call "problem-solving leadership?" That's leadership that moves from one problem, one crisis,

to another.

Find now, today, in your profession/work the good in what you do and how you do it and the ways in which you make others' lives better. Do it now. Do you like everything about what you do daily in your vocation? Perhaps not. Despite that, serve others!

Remember, it is our thinking that either stymies or releases the power of service. It is within our control to find a servant mind and heart, to find a means to serve others in what we do, to see ourselves as serving others, and to understand that everything we do is or can be a vessel for service. My thinking determines the outcome.

2. **Identify how you and your company are of service through your work and vocation.** Know that you serve others through your vocation, your work. It's already happening! In every vocation you see, whether it's a physician, an attorney, a barista, a mechanic, a hairstylist, or a server in a restaurant, people are making our lives better, just by doing their jobs and serving others. They are creating empowering moments every single day, in every profession and business, in every vocation. Do you see it happening in yours? Do you talk about it? Do you reward it? If not, let's get on that.

3. **Decide how you can be of service through your vocation.** Write your answers to the following questions:

How do I now serve through vocation?

Who is helped by what I do?

Be kind to yourself. Do not judge or punish yourself. Now that you have answered the questions, do you see the good in what you do? Stay open to the possibility that a power greater than *yourself wants you exactly where you are in your vocation.* Is it not possible that you were created for such a time as this?

Then move on to this: How would I like to serve through my vocation? What can I change in my thinking, and my actions, in my vocation? What more can I give to others in what I do, and to whom? What project can I implement in my company that will change and renew not only me…but the company itself?

How can I create a culture of service that will increase employee engagement, satisfaction, and retention; build our brand; generate free publicity that results in more customers/clients/patients; and help reduce our marketing expense with increased effectiveness?

A lawyer I know is an estate planner. He makes it a regular part of his week to visit (house calls—really!), at no charge, clients and former clients who are now confined to skilled nursing homes. First on his list are seniors who have no one who can or will visit. Frequently, this lawyer shares a meal with those he visits, complete with nursing-home cuisine. To a place often filled with loneliness and pain, he brings a great gift. He eases the pain of many. And he is changed, renewed, and empowered himself.

As the lawyer engaged in this wonderful service-driven

This lawyer shares a meal with those he visits, complete with nursing-home cuisine.

---

project, he began to talk with others in his law firm. He invited them to join him on some of his visits. Over time, the project grew to include most of the law firm, including paralegals, administrative staff, and lawyers. What happened to the law firm was truly amazing. A sense of a common mission developed, not just in the project itself, but within the operation of the law firm. This was not just a "feel-good" project, a feel-good proposition; it was great for business. Becoming of service as a firm helped build the company brand and generated enormous positive publicity. The firm became known for the project and became known not only as a great corporate citizen but also as "lawyers with a heart." The result? Employee engagement in the firm's work and its common purpose, bonding from within, a sense of team. Bottom line? Enormous benefit to those served in the community and enormous benefit to the firm itself. This effort resulted in moving people and the bottom line, including profitability, forward in a truly extraordinary way!

4. **Allow yourself to be newly empowered in your vocation**. We talked earlier about empowerment—about learning, as Einstein said, to live outside ourselves and thereby find deep meaning and great joy for ourselves, being empowered in service to others. This fundamental truth is no less true in our businesses. Let's look at how empowerment is brought to the workplace.

Imagine what would happen if you took into your workplace the meaning you've discovered, the power and joy that are now yours through the power of service in other parts of your life—in home and family and with "neighbor." What would happen to your work and your work product if you thought of yourself as worthy? And if you saw yourself as fundamentally good, as loving and compassionate, filled with the capacity to forgive? If you thought of yourself as good at what you do? If you looked for the good in what you do? If you saw yourself as being "of service" in your work?

This might be a novel concept to you, perhaps a naïve concept. But it is as powerful in business as anything you will ever undertake. As you begin to see yourself as "of service" to clients, customers, students, and patients, you will bring into your life a new energy, passion, calmness, and determination, and you will have an amazing impact on the workings of your company and on its productivity and profitability.

Love and Serve Your Family in Vocation

Another specific way to bring true empowerment to the work place is to embrace a fundamental truth about what you do and how you serve: the fact that in your vocation, you support those most precious to you. That support can be an enormously loving gift. Do what you do in vocation with a servant's heart. If you allow yourself that much—to love and serve your family in vocation—you will begin to experience a very welcome peace and contentment in that part of your life.

With acceptance of yourself and what you do in vocation, the floodgates will open. Not only will you experience new peace and contentment; you will find new energy, passion, and productivity in your work. This change in your attitude and thinking is a powerful concept. It is the power of service that blossoms and blooms when a business leader embraces it.

Consider this story about vocation involving a business leader and his daughter:

> A young dad was reading to his six-year-old daughter as she was going to sleep. The dad paused, and a far-away look came over him. His daughter noticed. "What's wrong, Daddy?" she asked.
>
> "Oh, nothing" the dad said. "It's Sunday night, and tomorrow's Monday."

"Daddy, you like Friday better than Monday, don't you?"

"Yes, I do. I don't like my work much."

The daughter thought about that for a minute and then said, "Daddy, I like Monday better than Friday. On Mondays, I get to go back to school and talk to my friends, and I get to learn cool things."

"You know, sweetie, you're really something. Thank you for that."

Wisdom from a six-year-old? Indeed. A six-year-old who knows at some level that life does not happen strictly *outside* of vocation, *outside* of the way in which we spend 80 percent of our waking hours, outside of the way we spend the substance of our days. She has learned, even at six, that vocation is a part of life. She knows at some level that she has a part in a greater work. She has not been created for naught!

But the young dad is not alone, is he? You've seen the studies out there that tell us that 70 percent of men and women in the workforce are not just disengaged; they "hate" how they spend their days at work. They dread going to work, feel they accomplish nothing, see what they do as meaningless and worthless, and feel "actively disengaged" from what they do in their vocations.

When on Sunday night the young dad thinks about Monday morning, he feels powerless and without joy, meaning, or hope. Consider this: How would the young dad's life be different if he discovered a way to change his thinking? If *you* helped him to discover that change in thinking? Helping others see their value is priceless.

What would happen to this dad if he truly saw everything he does—everything—as a vessel for service, including Monday morning and the way he spends the substance of his days?

If we choose—*and it is a choice*—to live in misery in our vocations, we are choosing to live 80 percent or more of our lives without, or outside of, the power of service, outside the meaning, purpose, joy, and empowerment of service. The choice to live outside the power of service and the choice to live in misery in our business lives *is* a tragedy that plays out every single day in many lives, all over this world.

You can change that in your company, from the top down.

Acknowledge Your Contribution

Think about your work and how you spend the substance of your days. Then think of it this way:

> *"A power greater than myself has created me to do Him some definite service; he has committed some work to me which he has not committed to another. I have my mission—I have a part in a great work; I am a link in a chain, a bond of connection between persons. He has not created me for naught."* —Cardinal John Henry Newman (1801–90)

Now say out loud, "A power greater than myself—by whatever name I call that power—has not created me for naught!" Say this every day for a week, with your morning coffee or meditation, or both, and say it again before you go to bed each night.

"A power greater than myself—
by whatever name I call that
power—has not created me
for naught!"

Experience the meaning, empowerment, and joy that will begin to accompany you to and in your place of vocation.

If you want to take further steps in service through vocation, read pages 87 through 91 of *The Service Driven Life* book; there you will find six ways to discover your path of service through vocation.

One More Service-Driven Leader Can Change the World

As you begin to think about service-driven leadership and choosing to serve, think about the story of the dove and the coal mouse (both of these are birds; "coal mouse" refers to the bird's color and size).

A dove and a coal mouse bird sat on a slender branch of a tree in winter. "Tell me the weight of a snowflake," the coal mouse bird said to the wild dove.

"Nothing more than nothing," was the answer.

"In that case, I must tell you a marvelous story," the coal-mouse bird said. "I sat on the branch of a fir, close to the trunk, when it began to snow—not heavily, not in a raging blizzard—no, just like in a dream, without a wound and without any violence. Since I did not have anything better to do, I counted the snowflakes settling on the twigs and needles of my branch. Their number was exactly 3,741,952. When the 3,741,953rd snowflake dropped onto the branch, nothing more than nothing, as you say—the branch broke off."

Having said that, the coal-mouse bird flew away.

The dove, since Noah's time an authority on the matter, thought about the story for a while and finally said to herself, "Perhaps there is only one person's voice lacking for peace to come to the world."

This story represents what our work is about as service-driven leaders. It's not necessarily about world peace. But it is why we do what we do as leaders. *One more service-driven leader can change a company from the inside out.* And carry it to greatness. One more service-driven leader—like Bill Gates—can change the world, from the inside out, from the top down.

Make the choice to serve! Now it's time to tell others about your choice to serve—to inspire and motivate others to serve and to live a service-driven life.

Chapter 5

Key #2—Inspire and Motivate

"If your actions inspire others to dream more, learn more,
do more, and become more, you are a leader."

—*John Quincy Adams*

ey #2 to success as a service-driven leader is to inspire and motivate others to make things happen in a business. It is through this process that you will satisfy the "wakening in the souls of your workers a longing for the vast and boundless sea" that Saint-Exupery spoke of.

This action must come from the top, from leadership. It's what moves people, products, and services. One of the people who was best at inspiring and motivating people about new products was the late Steve Jobs. Remember the highly publicized and carefully planned unveilings in front of a live audience in Apple's high-tech theater/conference center?

Is the ability to inspire and motivate others a natural talent? To some extent. But it can also be learned. Every person who reads this is a leader; you have the power and the ability to inspire and motivate. When leadership meets the power of service, it inspires, moves, and changes people and companies.

How to Inspire and Motivate Your Leadership Team and Employees

Inspired and motivational leadership starts with a commitment to service and your communication of it. Here are four specific ways service-driven leaders inspire and motivate their teams.

1. **Model what you believe**—One way to communicate service-driven leadership is simply to model it. This will be natural and easy. Over time, it will become who you are. Having embraced the power of service in your own life,

you *will* be different at work. People might wonder what's up; and they will be strangely attracted—in a wonderful way—to this new and exciting you.

2. **Talk to your key people**—Share with them what you've learned about the power of service. Show them this book and the book *Extraordinary Living*, or send all of them, and yourself, to a Service-Driven Leadership Seminar or Retreat. Having made the choice to serve and undergoing change yourself, it's time to share the choice you've made and its power with those you lead.

    I am talking here about your key leadership, executive assistants, virtual assistants, public relations directors, marketing and sales directors, partners, associates, and other employees. They want to hear from you. Remember this: whether we know and acknowledge it or not, the universal human search for meaning energizes and motivates—or fails to energize and motivate—everything we do. Aligning what is important to us in the way we live our lives with something bigger than ourselves is absolutely key.

3. **Be of service as a company**—How about implementing with your key people a favorite service project of yours that your employees can participate in? Every great service project begins with a single idea, usually from one person. Why can't that person be you? Let your employees see your passion. Reward them with recognition when they do great things, go the extra mile, and put service above self.

You, as a servant-driven leader, are modeling and driving the very thing that makes your employees and partners feel

---

Every great service project begins with a single idea

---

purpose, meaning, joy, fulfillment, and worthiness. These qualities and feelings engage employees with you, with the business, and with the work. It doesn't get better than that.

Joint service, you see, creates unspoken bonds among those who serve. Service together, in whatever form or context, creates lifelong friendships, lifelong loyalties. In the foreword to Greenleaf's book *Servant Leadership*, Stephen Covey states that the old rules of traditional top-down business no longer work. "They are being replaced by a new form of 'control' that the chaos theory proponents call the 'strange attractor'—a sense of vision that people are drawn to, and united in, that enables them to be driven by motivation *inside* them toward achieving a common purpose."[1]

---

1   . Robert K. Greenleaf, *Servant Leadership: A Journey into the Nature of Legitimate Power & Greatness*, 25th Anniversary Edition (Malwah, New Jersey: Paulist Press, 2002), 3.

In Chapter 10 of this book, you'll find the story of a mentoring and tutoring program that changed the face of a certain law firm. The program brought its lawyers and staff together in a common purpose that changed the lives of those they served and the lives of those who served. One of the major beneficiaries of this service: the law firm's lawyers and staff became more engaged in the firm and more productive on the job. The service project itself helped build the company brand, generating positive publicity that cannot be bought!

4. **Tell them their value!** Another way to inspire and motivate your leadership team and your employees might seem obvious. But it's rarely done, and when it is, it's rarely done effectively. Tell them why the products and/or services your business produces are important and meaningful. You must begin by knowing that you already serve through your vocation and that you company or business is of service. It's already happening! If you doubt that, read this passage from *A Service Driven Life*, Chapter 5:[2]

> *Know that you serve through vocation.* A lawyer helps her client through a time of great difficulty; a gardener creates beauty in the lives of those who see his or her work; a pastor offers the congregant a place of calm in the midst of a storm—a life-changing and live-saving place. What about the utility worker who brings to

2 . Donald Clinebell, *A Service Driven Life: Discover Your Path to Meaning, Power, and Joy* (Oviedo, Florida: HigherLife Publishing, 2012), 87–88.

thousands of people the electric power necessary to their lives? Or the teacher who offers her students not just knowledge and learning, but role and success modeling and mentoring. The employer who provides jobs and thereby makes the lives of his employees and their families better. The employees who make the employer's business a success, create more jobs for more employees, and multiply productivity.

The worker in a fast-food restaurant who offers the customer food, but also adds a friendly tone and a warms smile. The customer, taken aback, says, 'Thank you for making my day a little better.' In that moment, in that corner of the globe, the worker is of service, the worker serves. It is a moment of power and of meaning. This kind of moment can happen and does happen every day; in every profession and every vocation.

Every vocation—yes, *every* vocation—is or can be a vessel for service! That includes *your* vocation.

Having thought about why that the service or product your business offers is important and meaningful, it is time to communicate that. *The art of communication is the language of leadership.* If you are passionate and empowered, it will not only show; it will energize and empower those around you. *Positive energy is contagious.* Positive energy begets positive energy, if you'll pardon the old English usage. And remember, negative energy begets negative energy.

Empowerment is contagious. Again, it's the *"strange attractor."* You are modeling a truly powerful and empowered way to live—service-driven.

Service-driven leaders are among the most inspired and motivated people on the planet.

What happens when we inspire and motivate each other? Oh, not much. Just exponential increases in energy, meaning, purpose, and productivity! Service-driven leaders are among the most inspired and motivated people on the planet. They inspire and motivate others around a shared vision, reflecting the wisdom to imagine and foresee what could be!

Inspire, motivate, and move others. You can do this *if* you allow yourself to be inspired and motivated by the power of service. *If* you remember that leadership comes not just from the head, but from the heart—*your* heart—you can indeed do this with company-changing and life-changing results. Think about it. Yes, *feel* about it and what you are doing. Pay attention. And prepare…which is the next key.

Chapter 6

Key #3—Prepare Using a Shared Vision and Goals

"Give me six hours to chop down a tree,
and I will spend the first four sharpening the axe."

—*Abraham Lincoln*

Now that we are service-driven, we must not get stuck in some naïve, generalized service haze. Rather, we are service-*driven*—as in what drives us to new, exciting, and perhaps uncharted territory as we "build our boats." We must prepare to change ourselves and the future of our organizations through a shared vision and goals.

Here's an old adage you might remember: "Advice for success as a leader: Be like a duck. Above the surface, composed unruffled. Below the surface, paddle like crazy."

The paddling is the preparation. What's new is that the paddling is no longer based on crisis and problem management and what must be "fixed" today; it is now based on purpose, meaning, fulfillment, and joy. You want to make things happen in your company? Prepare. Spend time with the "questions to think about" at the end of this book. That's a great place to start. Your preparation is not just found in your QuickBooks™ software and in your spreadsheets.

Your vision defines why your goals are important.

Again, spend time with the questions to think about in Appendices 1 and 2 at the end of this book. Remember that your vision defines why your goals are important. Coalesce around a shared vision with specific goals. What areas and issues in your company need to be addressed? What are the strengths? What are the weaknesses? Gather input, and set specific goals.

Perhaps one goal is to introduce your leadership team to service-driven leadership. How? Provide a copy of *Extraordinary Living* and this companion book on service-driven leadership to each of your leaders or to your entire work force.

Then, after giving them time to read and digest the information, spend time with your board, your leadership, and your key employees. Talk about service-driven leadership and about your shared vision for the company—the goals you see for the company and specifically for the leadership team or the work force, or both.

You can use the material in Appendix A for useful and empowering breakout sessions, with your leadership team and other key employees.

Perhaps your leadership team needs to attend a half-day or full-day Service-Driven Leadership Seminar or Retreat to create a strategic plan. Including visioning and goal-setting breakout sessions tailored to your company—visioning and goal setting that produce specific action items with "dates complete." These seminars force leadership to address the shared vision, set goals that will implement the vision, and force the production of the action worksheet and items that will produce results.

For more on retreats that are tailored specifically around the needs of your company and its leadership, contact the author or the Service Driven Institute Executive Administrator at theservicedrivenlife@gmail.com. Through the seminars or retreats, you can make sure that this book is not just one more book you read before moving on. This book and the revolutionary approach it presents can transform you, your leadership team, and your company. Our Service Driven team looks forward to working with you to create the format and tools your company needs.

Chapter 7

Key #4—Model Service-Driven Energy

"We often refuse to accept an idea merely because the tone of voice in which it has been expressed is unsympathetic to us."

—*Friedrich Nietzsche*

W hat is a leader's tone? It's not about being loud or hyper. It's about positive energy.

What's the opposite of positive energy? Eeyore energy: the monotone. Can you say the following out loud without sounding like the gloomy, depressed Winnie-the-Pooh character, Eeyore? "Hello. I love what I do. What a great company we have." Try it again, out loud, but with *much* more energy, and a smile, too.

Now, what's the most effective tone for getting and holding attention? Whisper. Energized whisper! Now, I'm not suggesting that you whisper your way through board meetings, staff meetings, employee meetings, committee meetings, and shareholder meetings. I'm suggesting that you need to *pay attention to the tone of your communication.*

You might remember a movie called *Michael* in which John Travolta plays a rather unorthodox angel. In the movie, Michael seems to know things about the other characters that haven't been told to him. And they wonder why. In one scene, he looks at one of the women on the team members staying at the Milk Bottle Motel: "I know why you're here, and it's not the reason you've said you're here."

Startled, the woman asked, "How do you know that?"

"I pay attention," Michael said.

When it comes to tone, *pay attention.* Whether you're aware of it or not, every time you take the podium, call a committee meeting to order, open your mouth at a board meeting, or simply talk to an employee or group of employees, you set the tone. You send a message. It might be, "This company is going nowhere, it has no energy, it has no vision." Or how about this? "This company is going somewhere. It's making a difference. It is in service. It's service-driven. It's growing, it's thriving, and you are going to want to be a part of it!"

That's service-driven energy. And *that's* the tone used in a service-driven company.

By the way, don't let the naysayers get you down. You know who I'm talking about: "Hey, everyone, Simmons here just uttered a discouraging word."

"Hey, everyone! Simmons here just uttered a discouraging word!"

These people need to find a way to be of service!

Your energy, your modeling, your shared vision will help them find it. A Service-Driven Leadership Seminar or Retreat can help.

Chapter 8

Key #5—Move the Bottom Line Forward

*"Only those who will risk going too far
can possibly find out how far it is possible to go."*

—*T. S. Eliot*

There are two "takes" that will move your company's bottom line forward. They enable you to implement the vision you share with your team and "awaken in the souls of your workers a longing for the vast and boundless sea," as Saint-Exupery said:

1. **Take action:** You've made a choice to serve. You've inspired and motivated. You have prepared. You've set the tone. You have exhibited positive energy, and you've done some visioning about the future. Now it's time to take action with specific action items, within a specific time frame. Spend some time now in Appendices 1 and 2 of this book.

2. **Take risks.** *Leaders take risks.* They seize opportunities to grow and get better as a company. Risk takes courage. I dare you!

The case studies in Chapter 10 are prime examples of taking risk.

The first one is about Mary Jean and "the service-driven software company that could—and did."

Mary Jean took what seemed, at the time, a huge risk. She gathered up all the employees in her then-struggling company and asked them to attend a Saturday-morning seminar. She asked them to attend, with her and with the entire company, a Service-Driven Leadership Seminar.

When you think about taking risks as a leader, look carefully at Mary Jean's story.

The point is simply this: from risk come powerful leadership and powerful results. Not just from a seminar, but from taking risks daily—risks that challenge you, challenge your employees, and challenge your company to grow in every way.

The second case study in Chapter 10 is about "the law firm that couldn't—and then could." The law firm whose team members began to think differently and then do differently and thereby found the firm growing in size, productivity, and profitability.

The third case study is another prime example of taking risk… in the small company founded in a residential garage that became a multibillion-dollar company.

Spend some time with these case studies. How can you use what happened in these companies and apply them in your business model, in your leadership, in your company?

Service-driven leaders—leaders who choose to serve—take action and take risks and thereby change companies from the inside out. They do it in seemingly effortless ways, in ways that produce engaged employees, in ways that become the *deciding point* between a company's enduring success and its eventual demise.

Take risks. Take action.

Chapter 9

Key #6—Enjoy Yourself!

"In all of living, have much fun and laughter.
Life is to be enjoyed, not just endured."

—*Gordon B. Hinckley*

Many would argue that this key to service-driven leadership—enjoying yourself—is a missing ingredient in most business leadership. Businessmen and women don't often appear to be enjoying themselves. Perhaps it's the pressure of producing a bottom line, the worry that if they relax for even a moment, one of the balls in the air will drop.

Sometimes business leadership carries with it constant and serious health issues: hypertension, heart trouble, diabetes, stress-related disorders, leaves of absence for mental or physical health issues, disability leave or retirement, early retirement. Does this key to success—enjoying yourself— provide a magic bullet for these nationwide problems? No.

But consider this: a sense of humor and of comedy, enjoying the lighter moments, and not taking ourselves quite so seriously are all universally acknowledged to increase not only good health, but to increase life expectancy and help "cure what ails us." I know a very successful businessman who routinely, when lunching in and not out of the office, will watch a DVD, or Blu-Ray, of an episode of the sitcoms *Seinfeld* or *Everyone Loves Raymond*. His reason is simple: "It makes me laugh, relaxes me, refreshes me, and makes me a more positive person during the afternoon's work."

Blur the Line between Work and Play

No matter where you are leading, no matter the venue, the

enterprise, the business—you must relax and enjoy yourself. That is easy to do if you start with a real sense of purpose, meaning, joy, fulfillment, and worthiness in what you do. That's the ticket to becoming a business leader who is blessed not only with a love of what he or she does, but a leader who is service-driven and empowered to work and serve—in a way that blurs entirely the line between work and play.

And that is going to change the face of your business, of your organization. Such modeling from the top is powerful indeed. It changes the tone of the company, or at least of your division or department. Service-driven folks carry with them a sense of joy and contentment that is very rare in business, or anywhere else, and is very contagious. Such leaders know that every day in our businesses, we have a profound opportunity.

I call it "the Edison opportunity"—the opportunity to make a real difference in service, with those we lead and work with, and thus in our businesses and in our communities. How often does that opportunity come along? More times than most are aware.

Step back. Take a deep breath. Watch a sitcom. Whatever you do, enjoy yourself!

Find Joy in the Journey

Back to those "balls in the air" that I mentioned in the beginning of this chapter. This image, more than any other I know, is at the center of many people's inability to enjoy what they are doing in their vocation, in their life's work. Remember, every business of consequence, of significance, of true purpose and meaning and fulfillment, has the stress of built-in deadlines, of daily demands, including employee problems and difficulties.

Every such business has ups and down; mistakes made, profits up, then down, then back up. Some of these difficulties and stresses can be changed. For example, employee engagement can be addressed and fundamentally changed. But some of these difficulties and stresses are simply built in and can't be changed.

So how, in the face of this, can we truly enjoy what we do? By becoming truly great leaders. By choosing to serve. By learning to inspire and motivate, preparing using a shared vision and goals, modeling service-driven energy, and moving the bottom line forward by taking action and taking risks. By becoming service-driven—and then enjoying the journey.

Remember, we as business leaders can't keep every ball in the air at every moment; sometimes a ball will drop. Or perhaps a ball or two has already dropped; we just think we've got all the balls in the air. That's OK. It's going to be all right. The joy—indeed, the purpose and fulfillment—in what we do as business leaders is found in the journey. The journey will end soon enough. Enjoy it!

Chapter 10

Move Your People and Your Bottom Line Forward— Three Case Studies

"Most men [and women] lead lives of quiet desperation.
And go to the grave with the song still in them."

—Henry David Thoreau

I have suggested that you have the power to move your people and your bottom line forward. One of the great joys of what I do is hearing the stories of companies and organizations that have done just that. Let's look at three. The first is my own law firm.

1. The Law Firm That Couldn't—And Then Could

For years, I managed my own law firm. For many, if not most, of those years in law, I lived in what seemed like a meaningless fog. Then I changed from meaningless and without purpose—simply surviving—to purpose: meaning, joy, and fulfillment When I changed, so did my law firm. And, shocking as it sounds, the entire team experienced real enjoyment and fun in the practice of law.

The following is a bit of my story as a lawyer, which transformed from a practice driven by fear and doubt to a practice and a group of lawyers truly service-driven.[1]

Think Differently

There are a lot of "yous" in this book. That's largely because I've asked you to ask yourself some fundamental and difficult questions and to examine service-driven living and leadership openly and honestly. Now it's time for some "I's."

---

1   . Clinebell, *Extraordinary Living,* 93–98.

I want to share with you how I learned to think differently and do differently, changing the face of my company and its outcomes.

What goes on between my ears? In the mid-seventies, I graduated from law school. Top schools, top honors, and then nineteen years of schooling came to an end at the impossibly young age of twenty-six. I was a lawyer. I found myself in public service with The Legal Services Corporation, at that time a public corporation delivering, or at least attempting to deliver, legal services to those who couldn't afford lawyers. Then, almost before I warmed a chair at Legal Services, I moved on to the California Attorney General's office, a Deputy fighting for truth and justice and fighting against oil companies.

There are, just in the state in which I reside, more than three hundred thousand active and practicing lawyers. Most of them, or so say the polling data, are depressed, cynical, and unhappy. I was one of them. I found myself working at something I was very good at but loathed. I disliked other lawyers, I disliked judges, I disliked the system—and I disliked myself. What I did for most of my waking hours was a means of financial security—nothing more.

Was there a God present in this? Did He care? Was I serving anyone but myself? "Surely not," I thought.

Despite my thinking, I flourished in "the law." I sued oil companies and won. I was promptly promoted within the AG's office. and in the early 1980s, I moved to the big money in a large law firm. Four years later, I opened my own law practice. My unhappiness grew along with my income. The world seemed

---

I had not yet found meaning in life—not even close.

---

a bleak, self-serving place. I tried to find meaning in a marriage, then another. And I watched, almost from outside myself, as "happily ever after" simply wasn't. There was the loss of a child through miscarriage and a failed marriage. I drank. I had not yet found meaning in life—not even close.

The powerful play goes on, and you might contribute a verse. Understanding service and its power requires an answer to an all-important question. What will your verse be? What will be the contribution of your life? Therein lies the joy, the energy, the passion!

For me, the reordering of my thinking did not come by lightning bolt; it came by quiet assurance. It came by a still, small voice. It came in moments of silence. It took work. I came to know my verse slowly, over time.

With the help of others, I began to see the very dark room I was confined in—by my own thinking. I had come to know a way of living that was focused not on my servant's heart but on a very dark room—both literally and figuratively—in the back of the house where I resided. I began to see the need for love and compassion—first for me.

What followed was, for me, nothing short of miraculous. As my thinking about "me" changed, so did my thinking about others. I began to truly understand and act on that phrase I'd heard so many times: "unconditional love for others," especially for my family.

One day, as I sat watching my young children play, I was moved toward something new, from what I now know was a spiritual place I had never known. I felt a quiet assurance. At that moment, I allowed myself a thought that was indeed foreign: "I am worthy. I am good. I am loved. It's going to be OK."

I make a living for those most precious to me. I now do it with a servant's heart. In my profession, my vocation, I help others and serve others every day. I make others' lives better. Do I like everything about what I do daily in my profession? Of course not. But that's OK. I still serve, every day, and I find great meaning and joy in that.

Early in my career, I worked in the California Attorney General's office. I was a Deputy Attorney General charged with suing oil companies for what were called "Reid vapor pressure" (RVP) violations at the gasoline pump. The results of elevated pressure at the pump are devastating to the environment; but the cost of lowering RVP is huge, and in some cases, the oil companies saw violations as worth the risk. I sued. I saw myself in some sense serving the "people of the state of California."

Then one day, a senior deputy, an Assistant Attorney General, began settling or dismissing cases—strong cases, in my view—for no apparent reason. I saw oil companies settling major violations with "civil penalties" that seemed like petty cash—funds it seemed were taken from the CEO's sock drawer.

Some very dark thinking appeared in me: "What's the point? What I'm doing is useless and a fraud." But that was fundamentally misguided. Will every avenue of service produce immediate and successful results? Of course not. Does that make me less "of service?" Of course not. It is my thinking that either stymies or releases the power of service. It is within my control to find a servant mind and heart, to find in what I do a means to serve others, to see myself as serving others. And to understand that everything I do is, or can be, a vessel for service. *My thinking determines the outcome.*

And the outcome of the RVP litigation was life changing for all of us; once oil companies did the "bean counting" and decided to stop paying civil penalties for excessive RVP, they did not produce lower RVP gasolines. They simply paid somebody to invent the rubber filters now required on the pump nozzles at California stations. That change alone, along with the advent of the catalytic converter, was instrumental in cleaning up the air in California. What I had thought was useless and a fraud was in the end of great service to all of us who breathe the air in California.

Over time, I came to reorder my thinking, simply to change it in a way I had full control over. I began to focus on service to my family, to clients, to those within my chosen profession. As I became service-driven, my law firm began to grow and thrive. Lawyers in my firm began to tutor and mentor kids at risk at a local middle school every week. Lives were changed, not the least of which were my own and those of the other lawyers in the firm.

For more on this program—7th-Inning Stretch Middle School Mentoring/Tutoring for Kids at Risk, "community service that changes lives"—see *Extraordinary Living*, pages 47–54.

Do Differently

As I began to reorder decades of negative and controlling thinking, it was time to take an honest look at my priorities. I had to ask myself, "How am I of service? How can I be of service? What are my priorities?"

My new thinking began to move me headlong into new empowerment, new passion, new purpose...and into great joy. My relationship with my children blossomed and grew as I began to see, feel, and act out of love and compassion in my home and as I began to see what I do every day as a means of service. By finding a means to serve others, including my family, in what I do, I began to find true joy.

As love and compassion for myself and others grew, I began to look for and genuinely want opportunities for service in the practice of law, both *pro bono* and for services I am paid for. I signed up to be on a lawyers' committee serving *pro bono* seventy-two United Methodist Churches in the Orange County District of California. I also signed up to sing in a praise team at a church in town, although at the time, that's all I wanted to do there: sing! My profession, and my leadership in it, led me to Rotary, the most accomplished *service* organization on the face of the planet. It is an organization in which leadership is about service.

I was moved—no, led—to have a hand in training some eight thousand incoming Rotary presidents during ten years of speaking and writing. I was moved—no, led—to found, and more important, to serve in the groundbreaking and multiple-award-winning 7th-Inning Stretch Middle School Mentoring and Tutoring Program for kids at risk. It is now one of the most effective and honored mentoring and tutoring programs ever devised for at-risk kids, and now it serves as a model for school districts and service clubs around the world. Lawyers in my firm and lawyers and businesspeople all over town now participate;

Lawyers filled with purpose are more engaged, productive, effective, and empowered lawyers.

---

they wouldn't miss it. Community service changes lives—of kids, parents, caregivers…and of those service-driven lawyers!

And for business leaders—particularly managing partners at law firms all over the world—here is the key: lawyers filled with purpose, meaning, joy, and fulfillment are not only happier people; they are more engaged, productive, effective, and empowered lawyers. There is nothing better for the bottom line than that.

2. The Service-Driven Software Company That Could—And Did

Once upon a time, there was a small software design company located in a small California town owned and managed by Mary Jean, a driven and energetic woman. The company was surviving but not thriving. Employee turnover was frequent, absenteeism high, productivity low, and the bottom line, in the words of the owner, was "scary." Some weeks, the scramble was on to "make payroll."

I ran into Mary Jean at a talk I was giving at a Rotary Club meeting about my book *Extraordinary Living*. After the talk and the question-and-answer period were completed, Mary Jean approached me and asked a very insightful question. She said, "I heard what you said about being of service in my life and about the change, renewal, and empowerment it can bring me in my life. What about my business?"

What about Mary Jean's business and her leadership in it? Intuitively, Mary Jean sensed the fundamental truth that "everything we do—yes, everything—is or can be an opportunity for service." The impact of service-driven leaders is powerful indeed.

I suggested to Mary Jean that she and I meet and talk about her company, its structure, its size, its issues, and the company's goals and vision for the future. We met, and out of it came the beginnings of a strategic plan. A month later, Mary Jean and all her employees addressed the first goal contained in the strategic plan: create a vision for the company and the goals to implement it. Mary Jean and all her employees attended a Service-Driven Leader half-day retreat, during which we addressed many of the breakout questions contained in Appendices 1 and 2 of this book, as well as some additional breakout questions tailored to Mary Jean's software company.

The day began with training in the power of service and service-driven leadership, and it ended with three things:

- A specific, written vision
- Goals with time frames for completion
- Specific action items, again with time frames for completion

The breakout sessions were indeed productive, but they were also inspiring and motivating in ways not seen in that company before. One leadership team member, an assistant to Mary Jean, led several of the employees in brainstorming about how employees feel about what they do, what's important and meaningful in their work, and how that makes them "of service." They also discussed how they could be more of service in working with customers and potential customers.

Then that same breakout session was guided through an exercise in how the *company* can be of service. The excitement grew and was palpable when several folks talked about how "cool" it would be to do a joint service project. Another talked about the possibility of the company actively seeking out "career talk" opportunities at schools with high numbers of at-risk kids. Another responded that she knew about a middle-school mentoring and tutoring program that they could all participate in once a week—together.

Much more happened that morning. We began with fellowship and words of inspiration at 8:00 a.m. and worked until 12:30 p.m. It is not overstatement to say that no one wanted to leave at 12:30. What was happening in the discussion of joint service was the beginning of unspoken bonds, of true engagement with each other and with the company.

In a separate breakout session with Mary Jean and her administrative assistant, we explored the six keys to success contained in this book. Specifically, we talked about making the choice to serve, about the four fundamental principles of service-driven leadership (Key #1):

Examine what you do and how you do it.

Identify how you and your company are of service. ("We're not" was taken off the table as an acceptable answer!)

Decide how you want to be of service and how you want your company to be of service.

Allow yourself to be newly empowered in service-driven leadership and vocation.

The leadership team and I ended our breakouts with the keys to inspiring and motivating our people (Key #2):

- The "strange attractor"—what it is and how to use it
- The importance of talking to your people
- How to be of service as a company
- Why you should tell them of their value

At approximately 11:30 a.m., we held a plenary session, bringing all the participants together as a team to talk about the morning, the vision and goals, and the next steps.

The retreat ended officially around 12:30 p.m. But one employee and Mary Jean stayed until close to 2:00 p.m. Again, the excitement was palpable. There were many smiles; bonds had been created; vision and goals were developed; action items were created, with exciting and specific proposed changes in work environment, practices, and procedures; and specific service projects were discussed and embraced. The tone was set. It was time to take risks and to take action!

As Mary Jean left the room, she smiled and said, "I feel changed, renewed, and empowered already! I can't wait to get to the office on Monday!" Within a few weeks, Mary Jean had started a mentoring and tutoring program sponsored by her company. At first, a few employees attended, and then a few more. Over time, the company became known for its commitment to middle-school mentoring and tutoring of kids at risk. And what did that mean? Only this: that this service-driven software company

---

The company became known for its commitment to middle-school mentoring and tutoring of kids at risk.

---

was engaged in a common purpose that changed the lives of those they served and the lives of those *who* served. One of the major beneficiaries of this service: the company. The leadership and the employees became more engaged in the company and more productive on the job. The service project itself helped build the company brand, generating enormous positive energy and publicity. It was marketing of the best kind, marketing and publicity that moved the bottom line forward in a big way.

Nine months after the seminar, Mary Jean wrote this note to me:

Thanks, Donald, for your amazing leadership seminar with us. In half a day, we were energized, inspired, and changed forever. This is not hyperbole. The change in the engagement of our leadership, and increasingly in our employees, has been a joy to watch. And not bad for the bottom line! Can't thank you enough!

3. Microsoft: Moving the Bottom Line

Let's revisit Bill Gates and that now multinational company, Microsoft, headquartered in Redmond, Washington. Some would argue that the unparalleled success of Microsoft was because of the brilliance of Bill Gates and a couple of other individuals. The business that started in a garage now deals in bottom lines in the hundreds of millions. Gates is worth billions of dollars.

Brilliance is good for success and can be important. But for every brilliant and financially successful business leader, there is an equally unsuccessful business leader. Part of the key to the success of Microsoft was Gates's leadership. Whether he knew it or not, he made the choice to serve. That choice was, and is, the key to his greatness. His attitude of service gave him the power to shape the future with Microsoft and later with a charitable foundation. That choice was, I believe, not made at the time of forming the charitable foundation. *It was made at the time of founding Microsoft.* A culture of service with all its benefits was built into the company from the very start, in that small garage in Albuquerque, New Mexico.

Like Edison, the technology Gates found and invented while at Microsoft has not and will not be fully utilized till long after Gates is gone. He has said that. And having been of service to a world now filled with technology, Gates devotes all of this time to the Bill and Melinda Gates Charitable Foundation.

These are just three examples of companies that have been changed from the inside out by service-driven leaders. They changed at the bottom line; improved their productivity and engagement; and renewed their purpose, meaning, joy, worthiness, and fulfillment. They awakened the longing in the souls of their most valuable resource—their people.

Remember, the greatness of service-driven leaders lies in their ability to produce engaged employees—those who are inspired and motivated—and employees who are involved in, enthusiastic about, and committed to their work and to their company's vision and future. Outlook changes outcomes!

Chapter 11

"Too Busy" Is a Myth

"Beware the barrenness of a busy life."

—Socrates

A t a recent seminar I conducted, a young and vibrant man approached me during a break. He carried with him several devices—cell phone, Apple laptop, and notebook. He seemed engaged on all three of those devices as he spoke with me. The man identified himself as a CEO of a large but struggling manufacturing company. As he manipulated his electronic devices, he spoke to me: "This stuff sounds good, but I simply don't have time to do it all. I'm too busy."

My reply was, "Perhaps it is time to take a look at what's really important."

"Too busy" is a myth. We make time for what's important to us. We start with this premise, and we take it to two places:

1. **Apply the principles now**—If you really want to change the outcomes in your organization, you must work now on the practical application of the power of service, even if it seems to you at this point naïve, time-consuming, or both. Use the concepts and principles of service-driven leadership contained in this book.

2. **Lead the way**—If you think it is too time-consuming to learn to truly be of service, and to learn how to change the face of your company and your business, you must change that thinking now, today. If you want to discover purpose, meaning, joy, fulfillment, worthiness, and peace, *you* must be service-driven. Remember, the great leader is seen as service-driven first, and that simple fact is the key to his or her greatness. To be truly great, your company must have

service-driven leadership.

If you decide today that you want to take action toward becoming a service-driven leader, you will have decided to make some changes in yourself—changes that take courage but have an enormous payoff. You will have decided to change fundamentally how your company operates from within and how it presents itself to the world at large, including to your customers and clients. This takes some time and dynamic leadership; for many, it involves some fundamental realigning and reordering of thinking and actions. But the new energy, vision, engagement, and thus productivity that will begin to emerge in your company will be evident almost immediately.

Carl Jung once said that "to be normal is the ideal aim of the unsuccessful." If you want to be "normal," with business as usual, you can certainly stay with the old school, the leadership practices preached for a hundred years. But to do so would be to profoundly limit your leadership capacity. You are not too busy for greatness. Your company is ready for greatness. Now is the time for service-driven success!

Chapter 12

Leadership in Business—Not Just Another Theory

"Leadership is a choice, not a position."

—Stephen Covey

When Robert K. Greenleaf's book *Servant Leadership* was published in 1977, the concept sounded great. What was lacking, in the eyes of most critics, was how servant leadership would work in American businesses and those elsewhere.

Greenleaf, for his part, seemed content to focus on the impact of servant leaders on American and world "institutions," which kept any application of his ideas pretty much confined to academia and think tanks. In his chapter on "Servant Leadership in Business," Greenleaf focused on a "new ethic" in business— service-based—that could change the face of American institutions and thus could change the world.

All of that was new, but it seemed, at best, impractical and, at worst, obtuse. It failed to address the effects of servant leadership on businesses themselves or on business leaders themselves. Little attention was given to the potentially favorable impact on the bottom lines of companies that implemented servant leadership or *how that could be accomplished.*

Obtuseness creates inaction and changes nothing.

In 2011, Joseph Jaworski published his best-selling book *Synchronicity, The Inner Path of Leadership.* The book chronicled the author's personal journey from successful lawyer to a man fully engaged not only in studying leadership but living a deeply personal vision of servant leadership. This is a wonderful book that, in the words of Lois Farfel Stark, "teaches us how to recognize and respond to our own moments of inner knowing and how these personal shifts can reverberate in the world."

But again, if a you seek specific guidance about how the concept of servant leadership can move people and the bottom line forward in business, you will be disappointed in the works of Greenleaf. Obtuseness creates inaction and changes nothing.

My book *Extraordinary Living* and this companion, *The Service Driven Leader*, are intended to provide specific guidance. They answer the questions "How does this work?" and "Why does it work?" to change the face of business ventures in these times. From general propositions to specifics, it explains how to move beyond business as usual.

Stephen Covey recently progressed the discussion in his foreword to the Anniversary Edition of Greenleaf's *Servant Leadership* book. He points out, correctly, that "leader" has become a synonym for "boss." That is disempowering. The very top people in all truly great organizations are servant leaders. As Greenleaf wrote, "The great leader is seen as servant first, and that simple fact is the key to his greatness."[1]

What we have now learned, and you can apply, is that this kind of empowerment is what servant leadership represents. It is one

---

1 . "He Was a Servant First, a Servant at Heart," Robert K. Greenleaf Center for Servant Leadership, June 6, 2017, https://www.greenleaf.org/servant-first-servant-heart/.

of the key principles that, based on practice, not talk, will be the "deciding point between an organization's enduring success or its eventual demise."

There was a time when experts on leadership told us that presidents and CEOs should come from the sales, manufacturing, and financial ranks of a company. Now we know that no longer works. To ensure enduring growth and success, business leadership must include men and women of service—those who understand the power of service to change their own lives and the lives of those around them. Men and women challenged, moved, and motivated to be the people, the leaders, who "make their mark," not just on a spreadsheet but on human hearts and minds.

This is not just another theory of leadership. Rather, it is a choice. The most important choice you will ever make as an individual is the choice to serve—in every part of your life. And the most important choice you will ever make as a business leader is the choice to serve—without which your capacity to lead will be profoundly limited.

Extraordinary Living, The Service Driven Leader, and the retreats and seminars on service-driven leadership are designed to provide help with the choice. They also provide practical and proven strategies you can apply immediately to move your company forward. These strategies and results can change and renew you and thus your company, empowering and equipping you for the road ahead.

Chapter 13

A Postscript for Leaders in Troubled Companies

"Once you choose hope, anything is possible."

—*Christopher Reeve*

I f you are in a leadership position in a troubled company, this postscript is for you. Take heart. It's been said that a leader is a dealer in hope.

Here's the hope: the concepts and principles in this book are groundbreaking. If you spend time with them, they will move your company forward—in spirit, morale, excitement, creativity, imagination, and productivity—and eventually financially.

In a troubled company, with a troubled spreadsheet, becoming service-driven might seem counterintuitive—too naïve and not quick enough as a solution. Resist that! What seems counterintuitive is exactly what you've been looking for. It is a game changer, an infusion of energy, purpose, engagement, and power.

Think differently. Do differently.

Change is not an easy thing, and this kind of change requires some shifts in thinking and priorities. Think differently. Do differently. The first step is to acknowledge reality. Growth—in business, as in everything else—is not possible without first acknowledging reality, acknowledging the truth. In this context, the opposite of truth is denial. Companies that live in denial are doomed to failure.

Reality is not found just in the bottom line. It is found in a lack of visioning and goal setting, along with specific action items with timelines. It is found in creating that vision for your company that is now lacking. And it is found in leadership that acknowledges the "missing ingredient." You can indeed move your people and your bottom line forward in a way that makes your company truly great. But you must start with what makes you, as a leader, great. Be of service first, and that simple act will be the key to your greatness.

Go back now to the introduction, "The Missing Ingredient," and Chapter 1, "Seize the Opportunity." Perhaps it is time to gather your leadership team and devote half a day or an entire day to a Service-Driven Leadership Seminar. Perhaps you could benefit from a tailored retreat, with breakout sessions thoroughly prepared for and focused specifically on your company and its needs.

I can share from my own experience—and that of many other companies, organizations, and business leaders—that the investment in service and service-driven leadership has a payoff that most can't even imagine.

Please read the testimonials at the back of this book. From a small law firm to a medium-sized software development firm to a behemoth like Microsoft, the opportunity to move forward is there. Remember, you are not just building boats or ships; you are "awakening in the souls of your workers a longing for the vast and boundless sea."

It's been said that when it gets dark enough, we can see the stars. And when we see the stars, we move our vision, perspective, plans, hopes, and dreams forward. Take action now!

And in the wonderful words of lyrics by Sara Groves, know this:

> "It's going to be alright
>
> When some time has passed us, and the story is told,
>
> It will mirror the strength and courage of your soul."

> *[Copyright © 2000–18 by AZLyrics.com.]*

Appendix 1
Questions to Focus You on Service-Driven Leadership

(Facilitated or Unfacilitated)

Answer the following questions in breakout sessions or in individual study to get yourself and your team focused on service-driven leadership. The questions are categorized under headings that match the titles of the chapters in this book.

"The art of communication is the language of leadership."

—Anonymous

Seize the Opportunity

Do you see that logic will not take you where you need to be? Imagination will; leadership from within will. Leadership that comes not just from the head, but from the heart. It is powerful, productive, and inspired. It moves people, products, goods, and services. And it brings purpose, meaning, joy, fulfillment, worthiness, and peace to those who embrace it.

"Logic will take you from A to B. Imagination will take you everywhere else."

—Albert Einstein

_____

_____

_____

_____

_____

_____

_____

The Power of Service

To what extent do you see yourself as a servant leader? As service-driven? Why or why not? If not, can you think of yourself as a servant leader, a service-driven leader? What steps will you take to become a service-driven leader?

_____

_____

_____

_____

_____

_____

_____

_____

What is the value of the goods or services your company provides? How is your company of service—not just in contributing time and financial donation, but in what the company does? Before you answer, remember this:

> *"The great leader is seen as servant first, and that simple fact*
> *is the key to his greatness."*
>
> —*Robert Greenleaf*

_____

_____

_____

_____

_____

_____

_____

_____

Energy and Vision Drive Leadership

What is your vision of your company, where it is, and where it could be?

_____

_____

_____

_____

_____

_____

_____

Where do you see your company in five years? Ten? What excites you about that?

_____

_____

_____

_____

_____

_____

_____

Why will your company not only survive, but thrive and grow in empowerment?

_____

_____

_____

_____

_____

_____

_____

_____

_____

How do you communicate your vision to your employees, especially those who report directly to you? Do you communicate in a way that empowers—that uplifts, deals in hope, and makes those around you better? Or do you communicate in a way that disempowers—that deprives of power, authority, or influence; makes weak, ineffectual, or unimportant? If the latter, are you willing to think differently? To act differently?

_____

_____

_____

_____

_____

Key #1—Choose to Serve

How many of your employees, if asked, would describe you, first and foremost, as a servant? How many would describe you simply as their boss? How many would say they trust you? How many would say they believe in you? Servant first, not power first.

_____

_____

_____

_____

_____

_____

_____

Picture yourself as a "servant first," even if you're not quite sure what that means. Does it feel frightening? Naïve?

Counterintuitive? Or does it feel, as Mother Theresa, described it, renewing? Can you embrace the excitement, the empowerment that is within you? You were born with it, and it is uniquely you. It is love, compassion, and service from within you. It is the very thing that sets great leaders apart, and it is the key to your greatness as a leader. It is life changing.

"I live as a servant and thereby I am changed, I am renewed."

—*Mother Teresa*

_____

_____

_____

_____

_____

_____

_____

_____

Key #2—Inspire and Motivate

To what extent do you have the "strange attractor"—a sense of vision that people are drawn to, and united in, that enables them to be driven by motivation *inside* them toward achieving a common purpose? To what extent do you tap into the motivation within yourself and others?

_____

_____

_____

_____

_____

_____

_____

Key #3—Prepare Using a Shared Vision and Goals

Have you identified a vision for your company and communicated it to everyone in the organization? A sense of vision moves people and draws them in.

_____

_____

_____

_____

_____

_____

_____

Do you set goals for yourself, your organization, and every employee? Do you build in timelines for those goals and get buy-in from everyone about their value? Do you measure progress toward those goals regularly? If not, how will you begin focusing on goal setting?

_____

_____

_____

_____

_____

_____

_____

_____

Key #4—Model Service-Driven Energy

What do you model to your employees? To your leadership team?

_____

_____

_____

_____

_____

_____

_____

Do you model service-driven leadership by your actions or by talking?

_____

_____

_____

_____

_____

_____

_____

Are you simply a person of goodwill? Or a person of goodwill who acts? Do you know who you are in theory, or experientially? To what extent can you tap into your service-driven goodness to sustain venture and risk?

_____

_____

_____

_____

_____

_____

_____

_____

Key #5—Move the Bottom Line Forward

What percentage of your employees do you estimate are fully engaged in the mission of your company and in their work? Would you like to see that change? What would be the impact of that change, of fully engaged employees who see the chance for purpose, meaning, joy, fulfillment, and worthiness? Are they attracted to those qualities and that modeling in you?

_____

_____

_____

_____

_____

_____

_____

Key #6—Enjoy Yourself!

What is it about your company that makes it an attractive place for men and women to devote many of their waking hours, other than position and compensation?

_____

_____

_____

_____

_____

_____

_____

Move Your People and Your Bottom Line Forward

Why do your employees leave? Most don't leave for lack of pay or advancement. They leave because they are not motivated, they are not valued, they don't believe what they are doing is important, or they don't have any reason to believe they are of service. How can this paradigm be changed? When can it begin?

"What we do for ourselves dies with us.
What we do for others and the world is and remains
immortal."

—*Albert Pike*

_____

_____

_____

_____

_____

_____

_____

_____

"Too Busy" Is a Myth

Do you feel too busy to work on the application of the power of service to your life and to your company? Take a look at what's important in your life and where you spend your time. Do you have time for new energy, vision, engagement, and productivity in your company? Will you commit a specific block or blocks of time to apply the principles of service-driven leadership and to truly lead the way in your company?

_____

_____

_____

_____

_____

_____

_____

What does this statement mean to you? "A decision not to embrace service-driven leadership is a decision not to be great."

_____

_____

_____

_____

_____

_____

_____

_____

Leadership in Business—Not Just Another Theory

When you retire, what would you like to be remembered for in your company? What will be the legacy of your life's work?

_____

_____

_____

_____

_____

_____

_____

_____

What do you think of this quote from Joseph Jaworski?

"Most people are not afraid of dying; they're afraid of never
having lived… of never having found a higher purpose…
something bigger than themselves. And of having never
stepped into that higher purpose and at least tried to make a
difference in the world."

—*Joseph Jaworski*

_____

_____

_____

_____

_____

_____

_____

What do you think of this quote from Robert Greenleaf:

*"The great leader is seen as a servant first
and that simple fact is the key to his or her greatness."*

_____

_____

_____

_____

_____

_____

_____

What do you take from the following quotation? How does this metaphor apply to your business, your trade, your company?

*"If you want to build a boat, don't begin by collecting wood,
cutting boards, or assigning tasks. Begin by awakening in the
souls of your workers a longing for the vast and boundless sea."*

—Antoine de Saint-Exupery

Appendix 2

Focus on the Keys to Success as a Service-Driven Leader

(Facilitated or Unfacilitated)

Use the following summary of the six keys to success as a service-driven leader in breakout sessions or in individual study. This exercise is designed to get yourself and your team focused on being successful as service-driven leaders.

Key #1—Choose to Serve

Consider the four principles of service-driven leadership. Talk or write about each. Include an honest appraisal of whether you currently act on the principle and what could be different. What needs to happen to make the principle one of the underlying strengths of your company/business?

1. Examine what you do and how you do it.

2. Identify how you and your company are of service through your work and vocation.

3. Decide how you can be of service through your vocation.

4. Allow yourself to be empowered in your vocation!

If you need help thinking about these principles, return to Chapter 4 of this book, which covers Key #1.

Key #2—Inspire and Motivate

1. **Know what the "strange attractor" is and how to use it.** Do you understand this principle? Have you seen it at work in your company? Trust in this phenomenon. Service-driven leaders are attractive and charismatic (in a good way). They are role and success models. People are drawn to them in ways they cannot explain.

2. **Talk to your key people.** How have you done this in the past? How could you do this in a way that empowers those you talk to and the company itself?

3. **Be of service as a company.** How could this be utilized in your company, to provide team bonding, and increase your employees' sense of purpose, meaning, fulfillment and worthiness? And in fact that drives them toward the common purpose, vision, and goals.

4. **Tell your employees why they are of value!** Do you tell your team and your employees why the products and/or services they produce are important and meaningful? If not, how will you do that? Try talking about it with a breakout partner. Don't simply talk about the bottom line, profitability, promotion, and -compensation. Talk about why your products and/or services are truly purposeful and meaningful, both now and in the long term. Perhaps what you do won't be fully used until long after you are gone! (Remember the story of Thomas Edison.)

And remember, every vocation is or can be a vessel for

service—including *your* vocation! Your employees won't engage unless you inspire and motivate them about why what they are doing matters.

Try making a short, energized motivational statement about what your company produces and why that's important and meaningful.

If you need help thinking about these principles, return to Chapter 5 of this book, which covers Key #2.

Key #3—Prepare Using a Shared Vision and Goals

Preparation is important in any business endeavor. The prepared executive always outshines the unprepared. But this preparation is different and revolutionary.

This key to success is about preparation based in purpose, meaning, fulfillment, and joy—not in crisis and problem management. Spend time now with the questions in Appendix 1. They will take you away from exclusive focus on preparation devoted to spreadsheet and bottom-line thinking—something you already have mastered. It's not that bottom lines aren't important. But positive and changed outcomes are dependent on changed outlook.

Prepare now for you how you will take the tools of this book and seminar and apply them to your day-to-day business leadership. Be specific. Apply the "app."

Goal setting is an important component of service-driven leadership. Spend some time in the "set goals" section of Appendix 1. See what feels right for your company. Perhaps you need a tailored Service-Driven Leadership Retreat on a Saturday morning. It will focus your team on a shared vision and goals to be achieved in a discrete period of time, as well as action items with specific timelines for completion.

If you need help thinking about these principles, return to Chapter 6 of this book, which covers Key #3.

Key #4—Exhibit Service-Driven Energy

Do you pay attention to the tone of your communication with your leadership team and your employees? If so, how would you describe that tone? Is it energized, positive, and motivating? Or does it sound like Eeyore on his birthday? ("It's my birthday. Nobody cares...")

This can be changed easily! Not just the paying-attention part, but the tone itself, once you become service-driven! To achieve the right tone, embrace the concept of "extraordinary living" described in Chapter 2 of this book.

If you need help thinking about these principles, return to Chapter 7 of this book, which covers Key #4.

Key #5—Move the Bottom Line Forward

Talk or write about the next two paragraphs, or both. How do they speak to you?

1. **Take action**—You've made a choice to serve. You've inspired and motivated others. You have prepared. You've set the tone. You have positive energy, and you've done some visioning about the future. Now it's time to take action—with specific action items on a timeline. Spend some time now in Appendix A. Talk about how to take action in new ways, with new purpose, meaning, and empowerment.

2. **Take risks**—Leaders take risks. They seize opportunities. They take risks to grow and get better. Risk takes courage. I dare you! Talk or write about risk-taking leadership. Is there some fear in that risk taking? How can you put a service-driven team around you, one that will "share the risk" as a support team? It can indeed be lonely at the top, as the saying goes, but it doesn't have to be. There is nothing more empowering than a team of service-driven leaders!

Key #6—Enjoy Yourself!

Let's hit this one head-on. How do you think of yourself? As a good man or woman, not only good at what you do, but as a good, loving, compassionate, and forgiving man or woman? As a service-driven man or woman, as a good and faithful servant? Or do you think of yourself as a hard-driving, unhappy businessman or woman? Hardened by time and a high-stress vocation? Doing what you have to do to rise in the corporate world?

What do you do when day breaks tomorrow morning, and

you'd rather not put your feet on the floor to face another day? Perhaps the song of the bird and the bark of the dog seem distant and angels seem a myth from childhood fairy tales. If life has lost its day-to-day joy for you, the answer is right in front of you, but it might be difficult to see.

Chapter 9 is about finding yourself as a service-driven man or woman living an extraordinary life. If you want to truly enjoy yourself, your life, and your day-to-day business tasks, you must discover that the power and meaning in life are found in service. Those who life service-driven lives find an enjoyment—indeed a joy—that few others find.

Return now to the ideas set forth in Chapter 2, "The Power of Service." That chapter is about you as a man or a woman. We begin in Chapter 2 to know extraordinary living: The power to change and renew others, and the power of service to change and renew and empower you! Having understood that power in our lives, we can then apply the power of service to our leadership as business men and women -- with amazing results. And with an enjoyment and joy immeasurable in its depth and dimension.

If you need help thinking about these principles, return to Chapter 9 of this book, which covers Key #6.

Appendix 3

Service-Driven Strategic Planning

Vision, Goals, and Action Worksheets

"The most essential leadership capacity of our time is the choice to serve; when we make that choice, we discover the ability to collectively shape our future."

—*Joseph Jaworski*

It's been said that "if you don't know where you're going, you'll probably end up somewhere else" (attributed both to Yogi Berra and to Laurence J. Peter). Strategic planning is important to businesses and companies of all sizes. Strategic plans generally help company leaders answer three questions: Where are we now? Where do we want to be? How do we get there?

This appendix is intended for use *after* you've completed the book *The Service Driven Leader*, after you've completed a Service-Driven Leadership Seminar, or both.

Strategic planning has become increasingly important for small and mid-sized businesses because economic trends have created a more competitive business environment. Knowing your company's direction is more important than ever. And creating your own strategic plan—for whatever time period is appropriate to your company—is critical because no one strategic plan is appropriate for all types of companies in every industry.

This model for Service-Driven Strategic Planning is designed to facilitate within the planning process the application of the service-driven ideas and principles introduced in this book. If you prefer a more classic approach to strategic planning, see Appendix 4.

This Appendix 3 is all about "*Service-Driven* Strategic Planning." This is where service-driven visioning, goal setting, and planning specific action items—with specific timelines and dates for completion—come clear. This is where you can truly shape your company's future.

Strategic planning in business takes time and in most companies is ongoing—a work in progress. You cannot develop a useful strategic plan for your company during a half-day or even a full-day seminar.

Service-Driven Strategic Planning Model

There are eleven steps in the Service-Driven Strategic Planning Model.

1. **Identify SWOT.** First, identify your company's strengths, weaknesses, opportunities, and threats. This exercise is often referred to simply as "SWOT." Include in this SWOT where your company and your leadership team are when it comes to service. Is the company service-driven? Are you a service-driven leader? How is your company currently of service? Remember that every vocation has a service component; every vocation is or can be a vessel for service. To what extent do you and does your leadership team choose to serve, inspire, and motivate; prepare using a shared vision and goals; model service-driven energy; move the bottom line forward, and enjoy what you do?

_____

_____

_____

_____

_____

_____

_____

2. Establish your vision for your organization or company.

Your vision statement describes where you see your company going in the next year, three years, or five years. Include the ways in which you'd like to see your company be service-driven. Remember that service-driven leadership puts serving others first: employees, clients, customers, patients, community. When leadership meets the power of service, it engages and inspires; it moves and changes people and thus companies. Outlook changes outcomes and gives companies the power to shape their futures.

Would you like to see your company and its leadership team choose to serve, inspire and motivate, prepare using a shared vision and goals, model service-driven energy, and move the bottom line forward? Then build those goals into your vision statement, and communicate it to everyone in your organization often.

Remember that every vocation has a service component; every vocation is or can be a vessel for service. (See Chapter 4, "Principle of Service-Driven Leadership #2.) In preparing your vision statement, circle back to the Four Principles of Service-Driven Leadership described in Chapter 4. Also include the ways in which you would like to see the leadership of your company change and grow as business leaders. Would you like to see your leadership team develop the most essential leadership capacity of our time—the choice to serve? Think about how your company and you can help your leadership team make that powerful choice.

_____

_____

_____

_____

_____

_____

_____

_____

3. **Write your company's mission statement. Once you have completed** your vision statement, write your company's mission statement in no more than four sentences. This is a concise statement of what your company is going to do and for whom.

_____

_____

_____

_____

_____

_____

_____

_____

4. **Fine-tune your vision and mission statements to make them a _shared_ vision and mission.** Restate your vision and mission statements in a way that you will present them to your leadership team and to your employees. The goal here is to energize and empower them about a _shared_ vision and mission. How can you communicate differently than in the past?

    The art of communication is the language of leadership. And your employees are longing for purpose, meaning, joy, and fulfillment, in what they do. In this kind of communication with them, you can increase both employee retention and employee engagement, and thus productivity.

_____

_____

_____

_____

_____

_____

_____

5. **Focus on your own service-driven leadership.** Does the vision you've described above include the development of your own service-driven leadership? If not, why not?

_____

_____

_____

_____

_____

_____

_____

_____

6. **Set goals to implement the vision of your own service-driven leadership.** Describe the goals you see as necessary to implementing the vision of your own service-driven leadership. Goals provide a way to measure success, a way to guide you in a strategy to "get there." This is about *implementation* of your vision and mission. Implementation

is where most strategic plans founder or fail.

_____

_____

_____

_____

_____

_____

_____

_____

7. **List action items to implement those goals.** What are the action steps you've learned about that you can take to reach your goals? List those steps as Action Items on the worksheets provided in this appendix, with specific dates for completion. The Accountability Worksheet can help you keep the implementation on track and identify the need for revisiting which steps need further action and follow-up.

_____

_____

_____

_____

_____

_____

_____

_____

8. **Build a team of service-driven leaders.** Does your vision for your company include a team of service-driven leaders? If not, why not? How can you make that happen?

_____

_____

_____

_____

_____

_____

_____

9. **Set goals to build a team of service-driven leaders.** How can you build a team of leaders who are focused on service? What goals do you need to set in to implement that vision?

_____

_____

_____

_____

_____

_____

_____

10. **List action items to build your team**. What are the action steps you've learned about that you can take? Enter those steps as Action Items on the worksheets in this appendix, with specific dates for completion (accountability) and for revisiting for further action and follow-up. This is a critical part of the implementation of your strategic plan.

_____

_____

_____

_____

_____

_____

_____

_____

11. Include immediate actions. List in the Action Items worksheets at least half a dozen "immediate actions." It is important to begin immediately, while these ideas and concepts are fresh and exciting.

_____

_____

_____

_____

_____

_____

_____

Action Items

**(Including team member responsible and
date of projected implementation)**

Immediate Action Items

30-Day Action Items

90-Day Action Items

One-Year Action Items

Three-Year Action Items

Five-Year Action Items

Implementation Accountability: Tracking & Follow-Up

Immediate Action Items: Date Completed

Follow-up:

30-Day Action Items: Date Completed

Follow-up:

90-Day Action Items: Date Completed

Follow-up:

One-Year Action Items: Date Completed

Follow-up:

Three-Year Action Items: Date Completed

Follow-up:

Appendix 4
Classic Strategic Planning Vision, Goals, and Action Worksheets

Some business leaders are more comfortable with visioning, goal setting, and listing action items in a more traditional format. Here is such a format. It's what I call "old school," and it's often tied to the classic definition of leadership, as discussed in Chapter 3:

Energy + Vision = Leadership

This appendix is intended for use *after* you've completed the book *The Service Driven Leader*, completed a Service-Driven Leadership Seminar, or both.

If you've already worked though the service-driven guided worksheets in Appendix 3, feel free to skip this appendix.

Strategic planning in business takes time and in most companies is ongoing—a work in progress. You cannot develop a useful strategic plan for your company during a half-day or even a full-day seminar. As you work on your strategic plan, keep in the forefront of your mind the enormous power of *service-driven* leadership!

Classic Strategic Planning Model

1. **Identify your SWOT**. Describe the strengths, weaknesses, opportunities, and threats in your company.

   _____

   _____

   _____

   _____

   _____

   _____

   _____

2. **Establish your vision**. Describe your vision for your company or organization. This is about where you see your company going in the next year, three years, or five years.

   _____

   _____

   _____

   _____

_____

_____

_____

3. **Write your company's mission statement**. Once you have completed your vision statement, write down your company's mission statement in no more than four sentences. This is a concise statement of what your company is going to do and for whom.

_____

_____

_____

_____

_____

_____

_____

4. **Set goals.** What goals need to be set now, to implement your vision and mission? Goals and action items are the "implementation" phase of a Strategic Plan; absolutely critical to the success of a Strategic Plan. Spend some time here!

_____

_____

_____

_____

_____

_____

_____

5. **List action items.** What actions need to be taken to reach your goals? Enter these action items in the worksheets that follow, with assigned team members and dates of projected completion.

_____

_____

_____

_____

_____

_____

_____

_____

6. **Build in accountability—tracking, assessment, and follow-up.** Use the accountability worksheets to track and assess implementation of the strategic plan.

_____

_____

_____

_____

_____

_____

_____

Action Items

(Including team member responsible and date of projected implementation)

Immediate Action Items

30-Day Action Items

90-Day Action Items

One-Year Action Items

Three-Year Action Items

Five-Year Action Items

Implementation Accountability: Tracking & Follow-Up

Immediate Action Items: Date Completed

Follow-up:

30-Day Action Items: Date Completed

Follow-up:

90-Day Action Items: Date Completed

Follow-up:

One-Year Action Items: Date Completed

Follow-up:

Three-Year Action Items: Date Completed

Follow-up:

Recommended Reading

Clinebell, Donald. *Extraordinary Living: The Hidden Power that Answers Life's Most Compelling Question.* Oviedo, Florida: HigherLife Publishing and Marketing, 2016.

Clinebell, Donald. *The Service Driven Life: Discover Your Path to Meaning, Power, and Joy!* Oviedo, Florida: HigherLife Publishing and Marketing, 2013.

Greenleaf, Robert K. *Servant Leadership: A Journey into the Nature of Legitimate Power & Greatness,* 25th Anniversary Edition. Malwah, New Jersey: Paulist Press, 1977.

Greenleaf, Robert K., *The Power of Servant Leadership, Edited by Larry C. Spears,* San Francisco: Berrett-Koehler Publishers, Inc., 1998

Jaworski, Joseph. *Synchronicity, The Inner Path of Leadership.* San Francisco: Berrett-Koehler Publishers, Inc., 2011.

Testimonials about Service-Driven Leadership Seminars and Retreats

"I wanted to thank you again for our leadership and visioning retreat on Saturday. It exceeded my wildest dreams. Those who attended couldn't stop talking about it. The combination of what service is all about really hit home, and the leadership portion along with the breakouts were nothing short of amazing!

"We have now appointed a leadership committee to discuss the input received and the action items with which we emerged. When I first discussed with you this this half-day retreat, I had no idea as to how meaningful it would be and how powerful for our leadership going forward. Thank you! Thank you!"

—Jim Colitz, president, Mission Viejo Rotary Club, Mission Viejo, California

"Thanks, Donald, for your amazing leadership seminar with us. In one half day, we were energized, inspired, and changed forever. This is not hyperbole. The change in the engagement of our leadership, and increasingly now our employees, has been a joy to watch. And not bad for the bottom line! Can't thank you enough!"

—Mary Jean J., president of a software development company, San Clemente, California

Testimonials about Donald Clinebell's Speeches and Talks

"Happened to be in Capistrano Beach, California, and heard the fifth in the series: "Go and Do Likewise!" Awesome message, awesome and outstanding! Best speaker I've ever heard. Go see him! You will be changed!"

—Jennine D., Capistrano Beach, California

"Best public speaker I've ever heard. Period."

—Frank J., Los Angeles, California

"Made me laugh, made me cry. Powerful message! Terrific speaker!"

—Deborah H., New York, New York

"Best I've ever heard, hands down. His preparation, his control of the room, his presentation were all tops. Witty, informational, to the point; wove the evening together brilliantly."

—Bonnie M., Rotarian, Los Angeles, California

"I learned so much. Thank you! There aren't enough superlatives for this presentation. Riveting, moving, life-changing."

—John M., San Clemente, California

"Amazing! Such a dynamic speaker!"

—Lee H., Irvine, California

"He has 'it.' Truly a great speaker. He talks with us, not at us."

—Fran D., Irvine, California

"Dr. Clinebell is such a great speaker! And, oh, that voice!"

—Branden H., Irvine, California

"Cannot express how deeply moved we were and how much we enjoyed today! Wow!"

—Barbara T., Irvine, California

My Notes on
Service-Driven Leadership

My Notes on
Service-Driven Leadership

My Notes on
Service-Driven Leadership

My Notes on
Service-Driven Leadership

My Notes on
Service-Driven Leadership

My Notes on
Service-Driven Leadership

My Notes on
Service-Driven Leadership

My Notes on
Service-Driven Leadership

My Notes on
Service-Driven Leadership

MORE ABOUT THE AUTHOR

Donald Clinebell, JD, PBK, is the founder and president of The Service-Driven Institute, whose mission is to imagine and foster a world filled with men and women living in service to others, in every part of their lives—through home and family, vocation, and neighbors. Service-driven people live outside of themselves and thereby discover deep meaning and great joy for themselves.

Donald is a popular speaker and published author. His first book, *The Service-Driven Life*, was released in January 2013 to rave reviews and the written endorsements of many in the fields of spiritual growth and wholeness, spirituality, and theology. The book is a powerful and moving exploration of the power of service in our lives—using Christian terminology and teaching. *Extraordinary Living*, released in 2016, is the follow-up to *The Service-Driven Life*. *Extraordinary Living* is a groundbreaking study of the power of service in all of our lives, using values-based spirituality.

A Rotarian for more than twenty-five years, Donald has been a frequent speaker and has helped train more than seven thousand incoming Rotary presidents worldwide. Rotary is the largest and most accomplished service organization in the world. Donald is founder and chair of the 7th-Inning Stretch Middle School Mentoring and Tutoring Program for kids at risk. It is a community-service initiative that truly changes the lives of kids, parents/caregivers, and members/tutors.

Donald was one of five individual finalists nationally for the President of the United States National Community Service Award.

He is a member of Phi Beta Kappa, a recipient of the Mary Ford Beacon Prize in Government, and a lifetime member of CSF.

He holds a bachelor-of-arts degree from Pomona College, magna cum laude, and a Juris Doctor degree from UCLA School of Law.

He graduated with highest honors from UCLA's Trial Advocacy Program. From 1978 through 1984, he served as Deputy Attorney General for the California Department of Justice under Gov. Jerry Brown and Gov. George Deukmejian.

Donald is the founding and managing partner of The Clinebell Law Firm in San Clemente and Santa Ana, California. As volunteer counsel to several districts of the United Methodist Church and a member of the Annual Conference Lawyers Committee, he has represented more than fifty local churches pro-bono.

A much-in-demand keynote and motivational speaker and lecturer, Donald speaks on topics including service, mentoring and tutoring kids at risk, the power of service, and the meaning and joy of the service-driven life. He is a UMC-certified lay preacher. The Service-Driven Life lecture/sermon series has taken him all over the United States and even to South Korea and Europe.

Raised in Claremont, California, Donald is one of three children born to Dr. Howard Clinebell, a founding faculty member at the Claremont School of Theology and a pioneer in the field of pastoral care and counseling, and Dr. Charlotte Ellen, an icon in crisis counseling and women's issues. He is the proud father of two grown children, Brennan and Tessa. He lives with Bonnie in San Clemente, California.

In Donald's words: "Service is no longer a question. It is who I am. I strive mightily to '…live as a servant, and thereby I am changed' (Mother Teresa)."

Donald's avenues of service include:

- Through home & family
- Through the practice of law, The Clinebell Law Firm
- Through writing and speaking
- Volunteer counsel to the Orange County District of the United Methodist Church and a member of the Annual Conference Lawyers Committee, representing pro-bono some 50 churches.
- Charter member of the San Clemente Sunrise Rotary Club (SCSRC). Donald served as President of the Club in 1995-96. During his tenure, the SCSRC grew in membership by a full 75% and won seven District-wide awards and two international awards.
- Assistant Governor, District 5320, Rotary International.

Donald is a frequent keynote speaker at Rotary events.

- Featured speaker and trainer at Presidents Elect Training Seminar (PETS)—annual training seminar for incoming Rotary Presidents. In that capacity, Mr. Clinebell has had a major hand in training nearly 8,000 Rotary Presidents.

- Founding Chair of the 7th-Inning Stretch Middle School Mentoring & Tutoring Program for kids at risk. Founded in 1995, the program has touched the lives of thousands of kids. Community service that truly changes lives—the lives of the students, of the parents/caregivers, and the lives of the mentors and tutors. The program has received multiple awards, including the California Golden Bell, a statewide award recognizing excellence in community-based school programs. To learn more about the program, please visit http://articles.ocregister.com/2006-03-17/cities/24776692_1_rotarians-program-rotary-international.

- Member of the San Clemente Dons, a service organization whose membership is made up of honored and respected civic leaders.

- Multiple Paul Harris Fellow and Paul Harris Society Member (recognizing contributions to the Rotary International Foundation, which Foundation has funded over two billion polio vaccines since 1987).

- Praise Team (vocal) member: Palisades United Methodist Church & St. Andrews by the Sea United Methodist

Church. Our Saviors Lutheran Church. Sunday school teacher, Third through Fifth grades.

- Lay Preacher and Minister, United Methodist Church.

Donald's scholastic awards include membership in Phi Beta Kappa, the Mary Ford Bacon Prize in Government, Pomona College Scholar, Life Member, California Scholastic Federation, Biography: Who's Who in California.

More in Donald's Own Words

"I am so richly blessed, in so many ways—through home and family, those most precious in my life, through "neighbors," those whose path I have crossed and will cross. In vocation, I am also truly blessed. I have been given a great gift: The opportunity to serve others through the law and the legal profession.

And now I have been blessed with the message of *The Service Driven Life, Extraordinary Living*, and with the third in the trilogy, *The Service Driven Leader!* May you be truly empowered, as you move your people and your bottom line forward.

THE SERVICE DRIVEN LEADER

Moving your People and Your Bottom Line Forward

www.servicedriveninstitute.com

IF YOU'RE A FAN OF THIS BOOK...

There are several ways you can help get the word out about the message of this book...

- Post a 5-Star review on Amazon.

- Write about the book on your Facebook, Twitter, Instagram – any social media you regularly use!

- If you blog, consider referencing the book, or publishing an excerpt from the book with a link back to the author's website. You have the author's permission to do this as long as you provide proper credit and backlinks.

- Recommend the book to your friends, business colleagues, leadership team, and key employees – word-of-mouth is still the most effective form of advertising.

- Purchase additional copies to give away as gifts.

ENJOY THESE OTHER BOOKS BY DONALD CLINEBELL

Extraordinary Living
The Hidden Power That Answers Life's Most Compelling Question

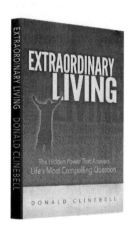

A loving study of the power of service in all our lives, across all boundaries of faith, no-faith, all belief systems and spiritual disciplines. Written from a values-based perspective, this book is all about true purpose, meaning, joy, fulfilment, worthiness...and peace, and the journey that takes all of us to that extraordinary place.

The Service Driven Life
Discover Your Path to Meaning, Power & Joy!

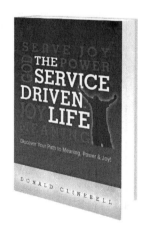

In *The Service Driven Life,* explore how faith sparks service. Written with extensive Biblical insight and a Judeo-Christian perspective, this book will provide fresh motivation and excitement to see how your spiritual life can be strengthened and energized in service – even as your life of service is inspired by your faith.

You can order these books from

amazon **BARNES&NOBLE**

or where ever you purchase your favorite books. You can also order these books from the author's website at: www. servicedriveninstitute.com

CONNECT WITH
THE AUTHOR AND WITH OTHER SERVICE-DRIVEN LEADERS!

Website: www.servicedriveninstitute.com

Facebook: www.facebook.com/donald.clinebell/

Instagram: service.driven.institute

Twitter: @DonaldClinebell

E-mail: theservicedrivenlife@gmail.com

INTRODUCING
THE SERVICE-DRIVEN
LEADERSHIP SEMINAR!

What if you could "make your mark" not just on a spreadsheet, but on human hearts and minds. That kind of leadership is rare – but it's possible!

This is a leadership seminar like no other. You'll come away with practical and proven strategies AND find yourself challenged, moved, and motivated to be the person, the leader, you've always hoped, even dreamed you could be.

If you're ready to move beyond "business as usual," this seminar is for you!

Join Donald Clinebell, author of the ground-breaking and highly-acclaimed *Extraordinary Living, The Hidden Power that Answers Life's Most Compelling Question*, for a half-day seminar designed around a most powerful concept: An approach to leadership that puts serving others first – employees, clients, customers, community.

You will receive practical steps you can put into practice right away. Your outlook changes outcomes.

Effective and engaging leadership comes not just from the head, but from the heart. And when it does, leadership becomes powerful, productive, even inspired. This kind of leadership moves people, it engages people, and, as a result, it helps you move more products and services with greater capacity and efficiency.

Do not miss this opportunity to re-engage yourself in your life's work and, in the process, engage your employees in what they do and why they do it.

To register and learn more about this event, go to:
theservicedrivenlife.com/leadership-seminar

SERVICE DRIVEN INSTITUTE

The Service Driven™ Leadership Seminar

What if your leadership impacted not only the bottom line – but transformed lives?

What if you could "make your mark" not just on a spreadsheet, but on human hearts and minds. That kind of leadership is rare – but it's possible!

This is a leadership seminar like no other. You'll come away with practical and proven strategies AND find yourself challenged, moved and motivated to be the person, the leader, you've always hoped, even dreamed you could be.

Discover a leadership style that not only moves your company's bottom line, but also moves you, changes and renews you, empowers and equips you for the road ahead.

A seminar that excites you about your chosen profession, about your life's work, about what you want your life's work to look like and to be; a seminar that excites you about who you are and what you do. And about your relationship with a power greater than yourself.

If you're ready to move beyond "business as usual" ...this seminar is for you...

Did you know that in most profit-based companies, more than 70% of employees identify as "not fully engaged." As a service-driven™ leader in your company, you will have the power to change that.

You will be introduced to 6 Success Secrets not found in most leadership books, including the power of service and a practical application of servant leadership.

Join Donald Clinebell, author of the ground-breaking and highly acclaimed *Extraordinary Living, The Hidden Power that Answers Life's Most Compelling Question*, for a half-day seminar designed around a most powerful concept: An approach to leadership that puts serving others first – employees, clients, customers, community.

Your outlook changes outcomes.

It is in this sense that effective and engaging leadership comes not just from the head, but from the heart. And when it does, leadership becomes powerful, productive, even inspired. This kind of leadership moves people, it engages people, and, as a result, it helps you move more products and services with greater capacity and efficiency.

Service-Driven™ Leadership gives companies the power to shape their future.

Do not miss this opportunity to re-engage yourself in your life's work and, in the process, engage your employees in what they do and why they do it.

The Schedule

8:00 a.m.   Get acquainted, coffee, continental breakfast.

8:30 a.m.   Welcome and Words of Inspiration

8:35 a.m.   Opening General Session: The Power of Service

9:00 a.m.   Break/Fellowship

9:15 a.m.   The 6 Keys to Success as a Service Driven™ Leader

9:45 a.m.   Break/Fellowship

10:00 a.m. Break-out session #1

10:45 a.m. Break-out session #2

11:25 a.m. Plenary Session (Action Items. Open discussion)

11:50 a.m. Closing Words and Sending

About Your Presenter

Donald Clinebell is founder of The Service Driven™ Institute, a distinguished author, a powerful and gifted speaker, and a true man of service. Donald has a passion for helping people experience the power of service and extraordinary living. He holds a BA from Pomona College and a JD from UCLA. He is of counsel to the Clinebell Law Firm and a former Deputy Attorney General for the State of California. Learn more at **www.servicedriveninstitute.com**

Donald's book, *Extraordinary Living*, has been called "groundbreaking" and "life-changing." "An instant classic." (Mike Darnold, PDG, Rotary International).

An advance copy of Donald's latest book *The Service Driven Leader* will be given to each attendee.

Attendees will also receive special discounts on his previous books.

You will receive practical steps you can put into practice right away.

Our Sponsors

The Clinebell Law Firm

Susan Dallas Hattan
Estate Planning Attorney

san clemente bath co

Shoffner Law Firm

In the
COMPANY *of*
PRAYER™

What others are saying

"I wanted to thank you again for our leadership and visioning retreat on Saturday. It exceeded my wildest dreams. Those who attended couldn't stop talking about it. The combination of what service is all about really hit home and the leadership portion along with the breakouts were nothing short of amazing! I had no idea as to how meaningful it would be and how powerful for our leadership going forward. Thank you! Thank you!"

Jim Colitz, Mission Viejo
(Businessman and President of the Mission Viejo Rotary Club)

"Thanks, Mr. Clinebell, for your amazing leadership seminar with us last month. In one half day, we were energized, inspired, and changed forever. This is not hyperbole. The change in the engagement of our leadership, and increasingly now our employees, has been a joy to watch. And not bad for the bottom line! Can't thank you enough!"

Mary Jean J. San Clemente
(President of a software development company)

To register for this event, go to: www.servicedriveninstitute.com/leadership-seminar

CREATE IN YOUR COMPANY
A TEAM OF EMPOWERED, PRODUCTIVE, SERVICE-DRIVEN LEADERS!

There is nothing more empowering than a team of service-driven leaders. How can you put such a team around you?

Perhaps it is time to gather your leadership team, or indeed all of your leadership and employees, and devote half a day or an entire day to a tailored Service-Driven Leadership Seminar or Retreat, with breakout sessions thoroughly prepared for, and focused specifically on, your company and its needs. Includes consultation, planning, and coaching with Donald Clinebell both before and after the seminar or retreat.

Let's move your people and the bottom line forward...together!

Like to know more about this surprisingly affordable and amazingly productive way forward?

To learn more, go to:

theservicedrivenlife.com/leadership-seminar

Congratulations on your work and your commitment, taking huge and impressive steps to move your people and your bottom line forward!

Want to increase your understanding of the power of service and extraordinary living in your own life and thus in your leadership? As a service-driven leader you are invited to add to your library a signed author's copy of *Extraordinary Living*, by Donald Clinebell at an exclusive discount. *The Service Driven Leader* is in a very real sense a companion book to *Extraordinary Living*.

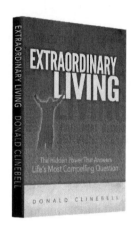

To take advantage of this special pricing for Service-Driven Leaders, just write to The Service Driven Institute Executive Administrator, at theservicedrivenlife@gmail.com.

I hope you'll include something of your story as a service-driven leader, and the impact of *The Service Driven Leader* book and materials in your life and in your business!

Many blessings...in love and service...

Donald Clinebell